Scarlet Stream

Unveiling the Mystery: Releasing the Supernatural

Dr. Sharon R. Nesbitt

Scarlet Stream: Unveiling the Mystery; Releasing the Supernatural
Copyright © 2015 by Dr. Sharon Nesbitt

All Rights Reserved.

Requests for information should be addressed to:
Dominion World Outreach Ministries
3700 Interstate 55 North
Marion, Arkansas 72364
www.dominionworld.org
info@dominionworld.org
Phone: (866) 579-5807
Fax: (870) 739-1332

This book or parts thereof may not be reproduced in part or in whole, in any form, stored in a retrieval system, or transmitted in any form by any means—electronic, mechanical, photocopy, recording, or otherwise—without prior written permission of the author, except as provided by United States of America copyright laws.

Scripture quotations from the King James Version of the Holy Bible, unless otherwise noted.

ISBN-13: 978-0-9962469-0-3

Printed in the United States of America.

To Yeshua Hamashiach,

Thank you for your shed blood.

Angela

Victory In The Blood!

New Doors of Favor!

Dr. Still

CONTENTS

Foreword – Dr. Vivian Jackson 1
Foreword – Rabbi Avraham Israel 5
Introduction 9

Part I: Revelation Of The Blood

1 | Nothing But The Blood 17
2 | At The Table 33

Part II: Restoration Through The Blood

3 | Gethsemane: The Will 51
4 | The Whipping Post: Physical Healing 65
5 | Crown Of Thorns: Wealth 81
6 | Nail Pierced Hands: Authority 97
7 | Nail-Pierced Feet: Dominion 111
8 | Bruises: Iniquity 127
9 | Pierced Side: Emotional Wounds 143
10 | From Golgotha To Galilee 161
Notes 176
Bibliography 182
About The Author 187

FOREWORD

Believers are often challenged to make sense of Old Testament types and shadows, particularly as they unfold in the New Testament. While reading, it can be difficult to tease out the shades and nuances of meaning that are necessary for understanding and applying the Scriptures.

In her book, *Scarlet Stream*, Dr. Sharon R. Nesbitt has paired revelation about Jesus' blood with principles of access to explain the power that has been given to believers. By tracing the role and function of blood in the Old Testament, she lays a foundation to articulate its culmination in the New. While some writers simply project platitudes, Dr. Nesbitt reiterates principles of actualization that both encourage and empower believers to live out the promises of the Holy Scriptures.

This book explains, in a practical manner, how the efficacious blood of The Lord Jesus Christ establishes our engagement of the supernatural. Although many attendees of Sunday School, Vacation Bible School, and regular Sunday services have been exposed to the concept of the blood that "washes white as snow," most have not been taught how to utilize the blood to operate in the supernatural and release the power of God in their own lives. Dr. Nesbitt uses this project to equip believers with that knowledge. By examining common misconceptions of the blood that are taught in the church, she teaches believers how to skillfully apply it with biblical command and spiritual authority.

No longer will the purpose and power of the blood be suppressed. On the contrary, they will be amplified as believers put to use the tenets set forth in this book. As readers learn how to appropriate the blood to every facet of their lives, they will tap into the *Scarlet Stream* that instigates a supernatural move of God, both in the earth and in His people.

- Dr. Vivian Jackson, *Hope Christian Church*

FOREWORD

"As instruments of righteousness, we are living demonstrations of faith, power, and the supernatural. Through the blood of Jesus and the faith of God, we are positioned in the Spirit to govern the earth as His extensions (hands)." - Dr. Sharon Nesbitt

Dominion is the first and only position that Adonai intended for mankind, and this book is an invaluable resource that can be used to help us apprehend that reality. In her book, *Scarlet Stream*, Dr. Sharon Nesbitt shows believers how to fulfill the Creator's mandate for humanity by charting a path of restoration. That path is made of the Messiah's blood and it always leads us back to the Lord's Table.

Full of spiritual insight and timely revelation, *Scarlet Stream* ties all of creation to communion. As readers journey through this book, they will understand why the Lord's plan of redemption cannot be separated from blood, and will grasp the significance of communion in Scripture and in their daily lives. They will also be challenged to resume the posture of fellowship that helps activate the dominion in which they were destined to walk. As they learn how to connect with Ruach Kodesh (Holy Spirit), readers will access the power of Jesus' blood, be restored to their godly place of dominion, and begin to carry out the finished work of the cross.

Though many statements in this book will grip the attention of readers, one of the most profound declarations is but three words—"It is finished." These three words denote the eternal accomplishment of the blood as seen in every aspect of creation and every part of man (spirit, soul and body). Such a weighty decree shakes us back into alignment with the will of God and summons us to comprehensive salvation. Now free to operate in the supernatural through ongoing communion with the Lord, we can access the scarlet stream that flows from intent to eternity, while using this book to manifest the miraculous in time.

- Yisrael Ben Avraham, *Etz H' Chayim*

INTRODUCTION

It's first Sunday. You know what that means. Crisp white linens adorn a sacred wooden table, covering the newly polished containers that hold the wafers and Welch's used to remind us of the cross. After the pastor reads excerpts from First Corinthians 11, ministers dressed in black prepare to serve The Lord's Supper. Immediately the room becomes saturated with sounds from familiar ballads like, "I Know it was the Blood," "Let Us Break Bread Together," and "Oh the Blood of Jesus." But music isn't the only thing filling the sanctuary.

Silent prayers of fearful congregants explore every nook and cranny of the holy space, stuffing the atmosphere with petitions like, "Dear Lord, please forgive me of all my sins and cleanse me from all unrighteousness. I don't want to go to hell. Amen." The air is thick and the mood stoic as the congregation approaches the Table. The wafer is chewed. The juice is swallowed. Inevitably, someone glances left and right and infers that the Welch's has started to become wine. Soon the service concludes and we all go home, still hungry for a revelation of the only meal that can replenish a famished purpose and restore a starved existence. Years of misconception encourage us to ignore the hunger pangs, but somehow, they just keep coming back.

Blessed are the hungry.

The pangs ruffle our dissatisfaction with mediocre living and urge to return to the Lord's Table. At the Table we experience uninterrupted, unhindered fellowship with God, just as Adam and Eve did before sin entered the world. It is there that we recognize the fullness of God's purpose for humanity and remember the blood sacrifice that enables us to walk in His original intent. The more we partake of Jesus' body and blood, the more we understand that communion is the center of life, not simply a part of it.

And yet, we cannot comprehend the significance of communion if we have not grasped the role and power of Jesus' blood. His blood is the basis of our relationship with God, the very foundation of our purpose in Him. So while we honor the death of Jesus, we realize that death itself did not restore humanity's relationship with God. Only blood could do that.

Because everything we are and all we are called to do hinges on the blood of Jesus, we cannot and will not walk in the abundance of God's purpose for our lives without a deeper revelation of it. To know that purpose and the God who created it, we must go back the Table, for it is the site of intimate revelation about His person and plan. The Lord calls us to communion not for the sake of ritual or image, but

INTRODUCTION

that we may know Him, understand what He desires for our lives, and receive power to accomplish it.

If you are hungry for what is only found at the Table, this book is for you. It was written to equip the saints with tools to reorient our minds, and therefore, our lives around the body and blood of Jesus. As we discuss the significance of blood in the Bible and in God's plan for humanity, we will see that it is directly connected to the supernatural. We will do so by unfolding revelation of scriptures associated with communion, the tangible demonstration of fellowship with God, and that revelation will prepare us to commune with Jesus in the seven places that He shed blood. After studying each of these places and considering their role in God's plan of comprehensive restoration, we will review resources that can aid us in strategically applying the blood to our lives and our lineage. As we learn to appropriate the blood of Jesus, we tap into the scarlet stream gives us supernatural access to Eden.

Scarlet Stream

PART I

Revelation of the Blood

The only guarantee of your presence, God, is your blood.

- Jason Upton, Worship Leader

CHAPTER 1

Nothing but the Blood

Something about it makes us uncomfortable, uneasy. Since we can't bypass it in scripture, we confine it to Easter Sundays and communion services. We've trained ourselves to avoid the blood. Like children watching a suspense-filled movie, we have learned to look away from all the bloody parts of God's story, not realizing that blood is our strongest link to Him.

Blood is a supernatural fluid that comes from God. A substance that no man can create, blood is also our divine connection to a supernatural life. When God put blood into Adam's veins (and therefore into ours), He placed life inside of physical bodies, for life is in the blood (Lev. 17:11). We first see the effects of this impartation through a change in color. Blood maintains a blue color while inside of the body, but immediately becomes red when exposed to oxygen. The color blue is indicative of heaven and red is indicative of earth (clay, dirt), thus, the shift in coloration signals a transition from God to man. Understanding this and other physiological components of blood will help us grasp a deeper revelation of the blood of Jesus.

Blood moves throughout the entire body to ensure that every cell is constantly nourished and cleansed. If it fails to reach cells or specific members of the body, they quickly die. In like manner, the blood of Jesus nourishes and cleanses us, and preserves our very lives. We see this preservation in the role of antibodies, which prohibit infections from ever occurring. Without them, the body would be overwhelmed with harmful contaminants that could lead to death. Antibodies remind us of Jesus' blood, and its preemptive ability to shield us from the final stage of sin, which is death. Blood also carries a host of information about our bodies and our lineage. Physicians can often determine what illnesses we suffer from by testing it, because if the blood is contaminated, the body will be as well. Again, we see a correlation in Adam, whose sin tainted the blood of humankind to such a degree that its poison continues to pollute the bloodstream of descendants over 6,000 years later.

But here's the good news: Before the poison was ever introduced, the Lord had prepared an antidote. His plan of salvation has always involved blood. Blood was in the mind of God before creation or the fall of man, because Jesus was slain before the foundation of the world (Rev. 13:8). Hence, the blood of Jesus was not a reactive plan employed to correct some unforeseen issue, but rather a divine solution for the problem of sin that was crafted before such a dilemma ever existed. Blood is so interwoven into God's plan for humanity that He repeatedly describes man as "flesh and blood" (Isa. 39:7; Jer. 17:5; Matt. 16:17). Blood has never been detached from the supernatural work of God (the greatest of which being the creation and redemption of all mankind), because His blood is the first sign of dominion. When the Father gave us His blood, He gave us legislative authority over the earth realm. As supernatural beings made in the image and likeness of God, we are ambassadors who have a mandate to access, inhabit and advance the kingdom of God among men by staying connected to His blood.

To stay connected, we have to comprehend the marriage of the blood and the word. Where the blood of Jesus is present, so is the Word of God. As the Lamb of God and the Word of God, Jesus shed blood before the world ever existed, laying a foundation of blood for creation and redemption. As the Word of God, He created us (John 1:1, 3). As the Lamb of God, He redeemed us (John 1:29). Since blood preceded creation, we were redeemed before we were formed. Therefore, we understand that the Word never existed apart from the blood.

Because the blood and the word cannot be separated from one another, the Bible is a living book. Hebrews 4 teaches us that the word of God is quick, powerful, and sharper than any two-edged sword, with the term *quick* meaning "living" or "alive." The Bible lives because blood runs throughout it like rivers in the Garden of Eden. God has set the cadence of our lives to the heartbeat of His word and linked our purpose to its pulse. It is impossible to walk in the fullness of God's word without grasping the role and power of Jesus' blood, for it is the blood that gives life to our teaching and power to the word. The blood is the power of the gospel that propels and validates the message of scripture. In fact, blood is the single most important prophetic word ever released in the Bible or in our lives today. When the time is ripe for manifestation of the prophetic word, Jesus' blood ushers that word from the heavenly realm to the earthly one. Our confessions, fasting, prayers, and faith are used to reduce hindrances of manifestation in and around us, but ultimately, it is the blood that allows us to see the prophetic word come to pass.

Every word that God released is an opportunity to exercise dominion, but we cannot rule what we do not watch. Watching over the words that God gives us, whether written (logos), spoken in present (rhema), or prophetic, means that we seek and apply the revelation of what He is saying. We refuse to lean upon our own understanding, and use with the blood to show ourselves ready for the manifestation of God's word. You see, many of us seek revelation and spiritual depth, but fail to realize that the blood of Jesus is the greatest revelation of salvation, deliverance, and the miraculous that we will ever receive, because *every revelation of the supernatural flows out of the blood of Jesus*. Where the blood does not flow, there can be no revelation. Our revelation of the blood (or lack thereof) is demonstrated in the way we live. Only when we begin to know God's word through a revelation of the blood of Jesus can we position ourselves for a lifestyle of communion. So we will take a moment to trace the stream of blood flowing throughout the Bible, finding revelation that will pour into us the very life of God.

The Scarlet Stream

Before we step into the stream, we should discuss the interesting origin of scarlet. The story begins with a worm (or maggot) that is pierced after it is attached to a tree. When the worm dies, it produces a red-like substance that is known as scarlet. Every offspring of this worm carries the same type of dye, and uses it as a defensive mechanism against predators. In Job 25:6, the son of man, a title repeatedly ascribed to Jesus, is labeled a worm. Like the worm,

Jesus is attached to a tree (cross), is pierced (with nails and spear), and ultimately dies, thereby producing a red substance that we know as blood. Through salvation, all of God's descendants carry this same blood, which is used for our protection and preservation.

We are reminded of the blood as we study Adam, whose name comes from the Hebrew word *adom*, which means red, ruddy, or to show blood (as in the face). Adam represents a red man, a connection that indicates a blood species. When God uses red clay to fashion the man in His image, He smears his body with the very color that would ultimately cover that of Jesus'. Most of us first notice the scarlet stream after the fall of man, when God kills an animal to make skins that will cover Adam and Eve's nakedness. God sheds blood after Adam and Eve sin because without the shedding of blood there is no remission of sins (Matt. 26:28; Heb. 9:22). Since Adam transgressed as a man of flesh and blood, blood was the only acceptable sacrifice that could provide mankind with access back into the Garden of Eden dimension of living.

God pronounces judgment after Adam and Eve sin, declaring discord between the serpent and the seed of a woman. This part of the judgment can be perplexing, since women cannot provide seed. Only men can do so. Besides, the woman provides no blood to the fetus because the father, not the mother, determines the blood type of the child. Yet, when we consider that Jesus is the only man born by the seed of a woman, the judgment begins to make sense. Because Jesus was conceived of the Holy Spirit, Joseph's blood never touched Him, so no Adamic blood was passed on to Him. If it had been, Jesus' blood would have been tainted, for blood holds our spiritual DNA and links us to our father. Born in sin and shaped in iniquity, our lives are permeated by poisoned blood until we are saved, or *born again*, which means that we receive new blood from our Father. So we see that birth is inseparable from blood, and understand that nothing we are called to birth (produce) can come forth without the blood of Jesus.

God's response to Adam shows us that blood had to be shed to appease His anger. Ask Cain and Abel. Both men were children of Adam and Eve who brought sacrifices to God. Abel sacrificed a sheep, and thus, shed blood. It seems that he understood that the only way to get to God was through a blood covenant, as mercy and grace did not yet abound. But Cain did not share this revelation, for he sacrificed fruit of the ground, which was cursed during judgment (Gen. 3:17). This explains why Abel's blood sacrifice, apart from being a tithe and faith offering, was more excellent than Cain's.

Scripture remains silent about blood sacrifices for sixteen centuries after the death of Abel, but after God decides to destroy the earth with a flood, we see the scarlet stream flowing into the story of Noah. He offers sacrifices of every clean beast to God immediately after leaving the ark with his family, and when God smells the sweet savor of this sacrifice He promises to never again curse the ground (Gen. 8:18-21), because a blood sacrifice can stop the curse. Moreover, God establishes a covenant with Noah, with his seed, and with the earth to never again destroy it with a flood. He even gives the sign of a rainbow in a cloud to remind Himself of the covenant He made. Interestingly enough, from heaven's vantage point, the first color of the rainbow is red. This means that red is the first color that God sees when He looks at the sign of the covenant, a holy agreement made only after the shedding of blood.

That scarlet stream eventually drifts into the life of Abraham, the man who would mirror in earth what God had done in heaven by a willingness to sacrifice his son. In Abraham's divine call and Isaac's miraculous birth, the Lord takes on the task of forming a people to serve Him. But His purpose could not be accomplished without blood. During Abraham's greatest trial, the sacrifice of Isaac, God teaches Him that divine life is only possible through the blood of a life in its stead. Because God had already entered into a covenant relationship with Abraham, the test of Isaac as sacrifice was also a test of Abraham's trust of the covenant. Isaac, the son of promise, would have to be surrendered to God, and death would be the only way to fully offer him.

Before Abraham attempts to sacrifice Isaac, he shows how the prophetic word is linked to a revelation of the blood. Long before Isaac is born, God announces Abraham as a prophet (Gen. 20:7), and Abraham declares the word of the Lord when he prepares to offer Isaac. When he sees the place of sacrifice, Abraham tells his servants that he and Isaac will go worship and return to them, despite knowing his intention to sacrifice his son. When the beloved son asks, "Where is the lamb for a burnt offering?" the prophet proclaims, "God will provide Himself a lamb... (Gen. 22:5, 7-8)." Abraham not only declares a sacrificial substitute for his son, Isaac, but also announces God's decision to offer Himself in Jesus as the sacrifice for humanity.

It would have been impossible for Isaac to rise from the dead on account of his own sin, for death would have justly held him. Nevertheless, the boy's life was spared because God had already provided a substitute in the form of a ram caught in the thicket, a bush of thorns. Since there can be no sin in the blood substitute (Rom. 5:7-11 MSG), this ram reminds us of Jesus, the blood sacrifice for humanity who was also pierced with thorns.

Four hundred years later, Isaac, in a very real sense becomes the nation of Israel. When Israel is delivered from Egyptian bondage, it is recognized as the first-born of God's children among all other nations. Thus, what the blood accomplishes for one person on Mount Moriah it ultimately achieves for an entire nation in Egypt. This happened as Israel began to see that God's supernatural favor, protection, provision, power, and fellowship came from a scarlet stream that had been winding through the centuries.

That same stream carried Moses as a man, like the Nile River carried him as an infant. In his early days, Moses flees Egypt to preserve his life after shedding the blood of an Egyptian, only to be commissioned to return there decades later. God uses him to facilitate ten plagues accosting Egypt, the first of which turns water to blood. Though this transformation meant economic vexation to Egypt, it signaled the beginning of economic deliverance for the Hebrews. The scarlet stream was setting in motion a miraculous wealth transfer for God's people. In the same way that God incorporates blood into the first plague, so He includes it in the last, not only with the death of the Egyptian first-born children (those born to rule), but also in the Passover. The Lord instructs Moses to command Israelite households to kill a lamb and place its blood on their doorposts so that the angel of death would pass over them. Hence, the presence of blood meant death for one people and life for another.

The children of Israel learn in Egypt, in the wilderness, and eventually, in Canaan that spiritual experiences are connected to the blood. Fifty days after they depart from Egypt, the Israelites reach Mount Sinai. It is there that God gives laws as the foundation of His covenant with them, which is established through a blood sacrifice. The blood is first sprinkled on the altar, then on the book of the covenant, and finally, on the people (Ex. 24:8). It was the covenant's foundation and power, because, as Abel seemed to understand, it is by blood alone that man can be brought into covenantal fellowship with God (Heb. 13:20). Adam saw this principle at work in the Garden of Eden; Noah observed it on Mount Ararat; Abraham learned it on Mount Moriah; the Israelites grasped it in Egypt and again on Mount Sinai. After sin, *no one gets to God without the blood.*

Adam, Noah, and Abraham witness the shed blood of animals, but that blood is never applied to anything. In contrast, the Israelites see the shed blood of an animal applied to the doorposts of their homes and eventually to the covenant. This progression of blood indicates a spiritual matriculation from person to household to nation, and finally, through the blood sacrifice of Jesus, to the entire world. The blood is most precious at the pinnacle of this progression, because the value of blood is known by the spirit that it carries (Matt. 6:26).

The progression of the scarlet stream is also evident in the story of Joshua, a leader whose spies understand that the blood is no respecter of persons. The spies make an unusual agreement with the harlot Rahab for her kindness to them, promising to spare her life and the lives of all in her household if she ties a red cord to her window as a signal to pass over her home. The scarlet cord, which represents the bloodline, does for Rahab's household what blood on the doorposts does for Israel. With the scarlet cord, Rahab binds herself and her family to the story of Israel, setting the course for Gentiles who would do the same in millennia to come. The agreement she makes with the spies is one of exchange, life for life (Josh. 2:14), and it foreshadows the divine exchange that would occur when Jesus gives His life for ours.

The scarlet stream also seeps into the message of Old Testament prophets like Isaiah, who points our focus toward Jesus when he declares the transforming power of blood: "Come now, and let us reason together, says the LORD: though your sins be as scarlet, they shall be as white as snow; though they be red like crimson, they shall be as wool (Isa. 1:18)." Though sins are initially likened to scarlet, after Jesus' blood is shed, they are utterly transformed. It is as if they are bled out, totally drained of their ability to stain God's people.

The prophet's declaration also attests to the potency of Jesus' blood, which is able to not only overcome sin, but also triumph over the voice announcing it. Those who have read *The Scarlet Letter* by Nathaniel Hawthorne know that the main character, who is accused of committing adultery, is made to bear a red letter "A" on her chest to announce her sin. Before the blood of Jesus, this is exactly what the enemy did to us (Zech. 3:1). He proclaimed our shortcomings, wrongdoings, and iniquities before God, knowing that the compensation for sin is death. But when the blood of Jesus redeemed and justified us, it presented us blameless before God and silenced the accuser of the brethren (Rom. 5:9; Eph. 1:7; Heb. 9:22). Now, instead of bearing the shame of a scarlet letter, we are born again through a scarlet stream.

Blood is the central focus of the Old Testament (also known as the Old Covenant). About 600 years before the coming of Christ, God promises the Jewish people a new covenant, which would also require blood (Jer. 31:31, 34). Both the Old and New Testaments (or Covenants) are ushered in by the blood; the first by the blood of animals, and the latter by the blood of Christ (Ex. 24:8; Heb. 9:18-20; Mt. 26:28). The animal sacrifices of the Old Testament are only a picture of Jesus, who is the conclusive sacrifice offered up in the New Covenant (Heb. 9:9; 9:11-12).

Reformation

Since the Garden of Eden, God has used a blood sacrifice to restore communion between Him and His creation, and the perfect blood sacrifice of Jesus allows us to operate in this fellowship. So while we do not seek to return to the Old Covenant in light of a better one, we do seek to return, in existence and operation, to the life that God ordained for humanity as seen in the Garden of Eden. The Garden of Eden is both a geographical place and a spiritual realm that represents abundant living. In every place that Jesus sheds blood, He provides reformation to and restoration of the original intent that God designed for us. We investigate sacrifice in the Old Covenant to understand and activate what Jesus availed to us in the New.

The Lord gives specific commands in the book of Leviticus concerning blood sacrifices for the atonement of sin. He instructs Moses to teach the priests what to do with the sacrifice in Leviticus 4:5-6, saying,

"Then the anointed priest shall take some of the bull's blood and carry it into the tent of meeting. He is to dip his finger into the blood and sprinkle some of it seven times before the Lord, in front of the curtain of the sanctuary (emphasis added)."

The priest sprinkles blood seven times, the exact number of places that Jesus sheds blood. It is sprinkled before the veil of the sanctuary, the very covering that is rent in two when Jesus dies. As the priest carries out God's commands in Leviticus, he helps prepare the way for the High Priest in Matthew (Heb. 4:15-16).

This revelation helps us grasp that Jesus died *for* us and *as* us so we might live *for* Him and *as* Him. The blood of Jesus helps reform us into the image that God designed for humanity as seen in Eden. That blood doesn't just save us from hell; it also frees us from a sinful existence, from mediocrity, and from purposelessness. We are loosed from these bonds because the blood speaks on our behalf. It reminds us of the conversation He had with Cain in Genesis 4:9-10:

> *"And the LORD said to Cain, 'Where is Abel your brother?' And he said, 'I know not: Am I my brother's keeper?' He said, 'What have you done? The voice of your brother's blood cries out to Me from the ground' (emphasis added)."*

Abel's blood wasn't just speaking; it was crying, shouting, and commanding the Lord to act (Heb. 11:4). And He did. In the same manner, the blood of Jesus speaks for and over us as the counterpart of God's word. Every word from God echoes what Jesus' blood has accomplished for us, and in turn, the blood gives us the ability to access and apply that word.

As we just stated, every physical place that Jesus sheds blood is a place of reformation that makes it possible for us to operate in God's original intent, which is to say, to operate supernaturally. The first feat that Jesus' blood accomplishes for us is salvation. When we speak of salvation, we must admit that many of our churches have not taught its fullness, but have rather restricted its purpose and benefits to "fire insurance." Not going to hell is certainly important, but escaping eternal damnation is only the beginning of all that the blood of Jesus warrants for us. God desires that we walk in holistic salvation, which is evident in abundant life and ongoing communion with Him. It is against His nature to leave anything lacking or incomplete, so salvation for the soul alone would contradict His character. To represent His nature well, we are to walk in salvation in every area, understanding that it extends far beyond the altar. Holistic salvation brings a healed heart, a renewed mind, a healthy bodies, a holy life, a prosperous existence, a good name, a realized purpose, a changed world, and a manifested kingdom. Like Rahab, when salvation really comes to our house, we, and all to whom we are connected experience total transformation.

It is *not* God's will that we suffer needlessly throughout this life to prove allegiance or worthiness for eternal life, but that we demonstrate salvation and wholeness in every area as a mirror of eternity. Some of us were fostered in congregations that equated suffering with true discipleship, presenting an image of the Christian life as one of living martyrdom. But if God's intent for us is seen in Eden, and Adam and Eve don't experience suffering until they sin, how can we return to God's original intent and still accept lives of perpetual, purposeless pain? To be clear, we are not suggesting that we will never experience suffering, for even Jesus learned obedience through the things He suffered. What we are saying is that every moment of His suffering was strategically used to strip power from Adam's tainted bloodline.

Rejection. Dishonor. Loss. Grief. Betrayal. Abandonment. Sickness. Offense. Misunderstanding. Death. You name it. He suffered it. Jesus took on every moment of suffering in the span of human existence and experienced the consequences of sin in Adam's blood to provide life for us with His own. The High Priest who was touched with our infirmities teaches us that, like a refiner's fire to metal, suffering is meant to purify the blood.

Jesus was tempted in every way, and was yet without sin (Heb. 4:15). Every time we resist the temptation to sin and choose to make decisions based on the word through a revelation of the blood, we keep the toxins of sin from infiltrating our bloodline again. We take on God's blood when we are saved, but every day we work out that salvation in our humanity, which is the part of us that was tainted by Adam's blood. When we choose to apply the blood of Jesus to our lives and our generation, the scarlet stream conducts a sort of divine dialysis that cleanses us and our lineage (Heb. 10:29; 1 John 1:7; Rev. 1:5; Rev. 7:14).

As we continue to apply His blood in specific areas, Adam's blood is diluted and that of Jesus becomes more and more concentrated. These areas are eventually saturated with the blood of Jesus and Adam's blood is made obsolete. We know this has happened when God's original intent is manifested in these areas, just as it was in Eden before the fall. So if you want to, as the song says, get back to Eden, you must begin with the blood. And to begin with the blood, you must first come to the Table. I hope you're hungry.

God became man so that man might become God.

- St. Athanasius, 4th Century Bishop

CHAPTER 2

At the Table

We're getting closer. Unsatisfied with a glimpse of God's silhouette, we move towards to the Table, to the place that we finally meet Him face to face.

Our pupils dilate to embrace more of His glory when the sudden clamor of misconceptions distracts us. They resound of our personal righteousness and disregard the power of fellowship with the Father, seeking to eclipse the radiance that we just beheld.

God sends a familiar voice to help us focus. It's Paul. We are comforted by his expressions, and yet, we fight to cling to words so familiar. Eventually we loose ourselves from the cheap satisfaction of finishing the apostle's sentences and ready ourselves for new revelation. Ears placed on the altar of circumcision, we listen closely for the heartbeat of communion.

Knowing God is the center of communion. Paul attests to this in Philippians 3:10 when he exclaims, "That I may *know* him, and the power of his resurrection, and the *fellowship* of his sufferings, being made conformable unto his death (Emphasis added)." The term that Paul uses to express knowing God (Greek *ginóskó*) is the very word that Mary uses to denote intimacy when responding to the angel, Gabriel. When discussing the conception of the Christ-child, she says, "How shall this be, seeing I *know* not a man? (Lk. 1:34, Emphasis added)." Both the apostle and the highly favored Mother teach us that communion occurs when our knowledge of God transcends information and becomes intimate experience. Constant fellowship with the Lord cultivates a pattern of intimate interaction that shifts communion from an event to a lifestyle. We transition into this way-of-life by inviting the Spirit of God to dwell and reign in every area of our lives. As Holy Spirit (Ruach HaKodesh) settles into these areas, He releases a grace that enables us to be *with* God, not just work *for* Him. Since God is most operative where He is most intimate, His blood is the greatest demonstration of His intimacy. Each time we remember the blood, we access the supernatural.

A miracle takes place as we partake of the Lord's body and blood. Because few of us learned this principle, we have unconsciously separated the miraculous from fellowship with God. Only now are we beginning to understand that God's original and ultimate purpose of fellowship is the impetus behind miracles, signs, and wonders. To know Him, we must come to the Table over and over again, for it is the place that God reveals Himself to us and shows us who we are. The desire to see Him face to face compels us to closely examine a passage that often accompanies our journey to the Table -- Paul's discourse on communion in First Corinthians 11. His text will frame the revelation of the Table that empowers us to live and operate supernaturally. Let's review it now.

> *For I have received of the lord that*
> *which also I delivered unto you* – (1 Cor. 11:23A)

Paul's discussion of communion opens with a transfer of gifts. The apostle knows that He can only give to the church what God has given to him, and that, only through communion can a disciple lay hold of an impartation from his spiritual leader. Every moment of impartation is an opportunity to fellowship with God and to learn the heart of the leader, but these opportunities can be missed if the disciple does not cultivate the spirit of communion. The spirit of communion is the consistent posture of fellowship that distinguishes proximity from intimacy. Exposure to supernatural revelation is proximity, but carrying the spirit (heart, essence) of God and of the leader to whom He called the disciple is intimacy. Without the latter, the disciple will misappropriate revelation and misunderstand leadership.

The disciple who communes with God and with his leader does not consider himself their equal, but commits to sharing in the areas that are opened to him. For example, if the leader opens revelation, the disciple opens his mind to receive. If the leader exposes areas of burden, he opens doors of relief. If the leader opens his life, the disciple opens his life too. This is what Elisha does. Because Elisha had the spirit of communion, he resolved to share with Elijah in every moment that the prophet allowed, and was therefore able to receive Elijah's spirit when he was taken. Elijah's spirit immediately directs Elisha to commune with God when Elisha invokes His presence and inquires, "Where is the Lord God of Elijah? (2 Kings 2:14)." Elisha's communion with Elijah equips him to carry the weight of the prophet's mantle of fellowship with God. We learn from Elisha that the disciple who asks for the spirit of the leader and seeks the anointing on his/her life, is dangerously foolish if he has not learned to commune. Communion with God is the womb of all ministry. Once ministry is birthed, the spirit of communion fosters the obedience needed for its alignment and the unity required for its advancement. Only then can we cultivate a new generation of fellowship and give in ministry that which we have received in communion.

> *That the Lord Jesus the same night in which He was betrayed took bread* – (1 Cor. 11:23B)

Do it anyway. This is the message that Jesus conveys when He prepares to sup with disciples, most of whom still don't understand who He is, and one of whom will betray Him before the night ends. The Messiah pulls Psalm 23 close to His heart and shows us how to commune in the presence of enemies. Eradicating every excuse for not coming to the Table, Jesus sits at the one prepared for Him and reaches for the bread. With hands surrounding the bread that represents His own body, He trains us to share ourselves, not only our gifts, with others. In so doing, He reveals the vulnerable nature of communion. The very love that makes communion courageous by casting out fear also makes it vulnerable to rejection, since fellowship must always be chosen. Despite His awareness of the betrayal, denial, brutality, and worst of all, separation from God's presence that He would soon endure, Jesus recognizes that self-preservation is not the mission of communion, and therefore still chooses to commune with the disciples, with us. However, Jesus also teaches us that every sphere of fellowship is not an inner circle. While He fellowships with many, Jesus reveals His divinity (Transfiguration) and humanity (Gethsemane) to only three. In like manner, we do not expose the totality of our being to everyone, but we are also careful not to withhold ourselves from others out of fear. To do so would be to hoard the very bread that is destined to be given.

And when He had given thanks, He brake it, and said, take, eat: this is My body, which is broken for you: this do in remembrance of Me.
– (1 Cor. 11:24)

Communion is God's story in a meal. Bread, the body representing Jesus' humanity, and wine, the blood signifying His divinity, remind us that heaven meets earth each time we fellowship with God. Every moment that we commune with the Lord, we tell more of His story with our lives, as we realize that He has attached our destiny to the remembrance of Him. Remembering the Lord through this meal establishes Jesus' blood as the center and framework of our mentality, and it brings alignment with God's original intent in our mind. We see this in the witness of the early church, whose members risked their lives for the faith. Gathering almost daily, these believers took communion and fellowshipped with God as if it were the last time, for it very well could have been. Always refreshing their memory of Jesus, the saints gained power to operate in the supernatural by warding off spiritual amnesia. While most of our churches don't gather this often, we must glean from the wisdom of the witnesses who preceded us. We learn to fellowship at God's Table daily, whether alone or with other believers, to manage the memory that allows us to apply the body and blood of Jesus to every area of our lives. After all, eating got us into this mess. And eating is going to get us out.

After the same manner also He took the cup, when He had supped, saying, this cup is the new testament in My blood: this do ye, as oft as ye drink it, in remembrance of Me. – (1 Cor. 11:25)

Meals in Scripture indicate, at least to some degree, communion or sharing. Adam and Eve's deadly meal in the Garden; Joseph's meal with his brothers in Egypt; the Passover meal; meals of the Jewish feasts; the Last Supper; Jesus' meal with the disciples after His resurrection; and the eternal banquet in the Kingdom of God all point our attention to communion, which always precedes a covenant. Covenants in the Old Testament could not be revoked because they were made with blood. Many of these agreements were so powerful that they impacted countless generations, as we see demonstrated in the life of Abraham. God established a covenant with Abraham and sealed it with 60 promises for him and his descendants. In turn, Abraham's circumcision established his portion of the covenant with blood, which was revealed only after the flesh was broken. Their covenant was not only an act communion; it was also an opportunity to co-create. When Abraham cut his flesh to symbolize a blood covenant, he created a scarlet stream that would flow throughout his lineage. Like a precursor to the Red Sea, this unlikely channel became the pathway to Abraham's prosperity and that of his seed.

The channel appeared to have all but dried up while the Israelites were in bondage, but they would eventually encounter a God who produces streams in the desert. As they cried out to the Lord, He heard the voice of the covenant made with Abraham and began to act (Ex. 3:16-17). God had bound Himself to the agreement and was, thus, obligated to move on Israel's behalf. His response to the covenant teaches us that God binds us *to* entities; He never wants us to be bound *by* them. Thus, the blood covenant binds us to God's promises; salvation binds us to a new birth (new blood); communion binds us to healing, wholeness, deliverance, and prosperity; and the scarlet stream binds our story to God's divine narrative. Because of Jesus' blood, we, like Abraham, are also in covenant with God and are heirs of every promise in His word. His body and blood keep us situated in the covenant's pathway.

For as often as ye eat this bread, and drink this cup, ye do show the lord's death till he come. Wherefore whoever shall eat this bread, and drink this cup of the lord, unworthily, shall be guilty of the body and blood of the lord. – (1 Cor. 11:26-27)

That pathway always leads back to the Table, but many of us refuse to come to it because we feel unworthy. That feeling can cause us to lose sight of what we know about salvation and righteousness. Satan, the accuser, reminds us of sins to reinforce a connection to them, knowing that if we forget that the blood of Jesus has severed this connection, the struggle with sin will continue in our minds even if it has long ceased in our lives. As long as we associate ourselves with the sins we have committed, we cannot receive a revelation of God's purpose or walk in abundance. This is why we do not call ourselves "sinners saved by grace." To do so is to partially embrace the covenant by accepting God's grace while rejecting our sonship. A full embrace of the covenant occurs when we come to the Table. By opening our mouths to take communion, we also shut the mouth of the enemy. Just as Satan is rebuked when he accuses Joshua the High Priest in Zechariah 3, so he is censored when we commune with God. Every time we remember the blood sacrifice that Jesus made for us, we surpass the sins that would have made us guilty because the blood of Jesus acquits us. Of course, this is not a license to continue in sin and abuse the grace of God (Romans 6:1), but rather a charge to understand how the blood of Jesus dismantles the power of evil.

If sin had the power to make us lose salvation, it would also have the ability to hinder us from ever receiving it, for we were all sinners when God saved us (Ephesians 2). Because sin has been overcome by the blood, it no longer has the authority to keep us from communing with God. Thus, the idea that we should abstain from communion after we have sinned is poor scriptural interpretation that fails to consider the purpose of Jesus' sacrifice. If God's desire is that we commune with Him and if Jesus made that fellowship possible through His blood, it makes no sense to break communion with God on the account of a sin already rendered utterly powerless. That kind of decision is therefore, not really a matter of sin, but of self-righteousness.

The desire to prove our worthiness for salvation arises when we parade the filthy rags of self-righteousness, despite the fact that all of us have fallen short (Romans 3:23). Because of Adam's blood, we have all dealt with a sin issue. Whether the issue was internal or external, private or public, seemingly minimal or severe makes no difference; every one of us would be hopeless without the blood of Jesus. None of us are righteous or worthy enough to get to Him on our own merit. Therefore, the issue of worthiness has nothing to do with our personal ability to abstain from sin, and everything to do with a refusal to ascribe enough worth to Jesus' body and blood.

In this passage, unworthiness means negating Jesus' ability to overcome the matters that seek to hinder believers from communing with God. It suggests that we deem Jesus unworthy to accomplish complete salvation, deliverance, healing, and wholeness for us. This sort of attitude of unworthiness manifests in many ways, but the most apparent is blind acceptance of sin and its fruits (illness, poverty, debt, chaos, inferiority, etc.). Many of us have unknowingly disregarded the work of the cross by tolerating works of the enemy, because when we accept anything less than what the blood of Jesus has secured for us, we call His sacrifice insufficient. Just as the blood speaks, so does the way that we live, and our lives proclaim not only what we believe, but also what we worship (attribute worth to). When we come to the Table and worship, we declare the sufficiency of Jesus' blood and celebrate His triumph over everything that would seek to encumber our communion with God.

But let a man examine himself, and so let him eat of that bread, and drink of that cup. For he that eats and drinks unworthily, eats and drinks damnation to himself, not discerning the lord's body.
– (1 Cor. 11:28-29)

Understanding unworthiness is essential to grasping Paul's warning against damnation, because it is directly connected to our capacity to discern the Lord's body. Many of us have understood damnation as eternal separation from God, a consequence no less than ironic if it results from fellowship with Him. Some of our churches have taught us that if a believer sins and takes communion before confessing that sin, he will be in danger of everlasting damnation. Therefore, it is not the sin itself that warrants damnation, but communing with God after it that sends people to hell. Such a notion suggests that the danger lies in fellowshipping with God, not necessarily sinning against Him. If this sounds alarming, it is. If it sounds unbiblical, it is. If it sounds like what you've been told, keep reading.

To be sure, the aim of this ideology is not to promote sin, but it does promote separation from the Table. This belief encourages people to guard the Table, as if it needed to be protected from a greater power, from sin. We know that Jesus eradicated our issues with sin on the cross and saved us from everlasting separation from God. How then, could communing with God after sinning result in the very outcome addressed by Jesus' sacrifice? Put another way, if God would convert a former murderer into an apostle who wrote the very text that guides our communion services, surely He would not damn a son for attempting to take part in one.

Examining this widespread view on damnation and its implications helps us understand that salvation is not the pivotal issue of this passage; discernment is. The consequence of damnation results from failure to discern the Lord's body, not failure to abstain from sin or stay away from the Table. Here damnation is not used to suggest eternal separation from God, for it is written to believers. Rather it means separation from the life that God has provided for us *in the earth* by damning up, shutting off, or holding back the blessings that come from discerning His body. We discern the Lord's body when we ascertain what Jesus accomplished for us and apply that revelation to our lives through faith and communion. Doing so positions us to access and implement God's original intent in *this* lifetime. So discernment, like worthiness, means that we neither accept nor maintain anything less than the comprehensive salvation, deliverance, and wholeness provided by the shed blood of Jesus. When we walk in the conviction that all we need is at the Table, nothing will be impossible to us.

AT THE TABLE

For this cause many are weak and sickly
among you, and many sleep. – (1 Cor. 11:30)

If sickness is a product of evil (and it is), why do so many believers suffer from illness and disease? Paul teaches us that sickness, weakness, and even premature death (sleep) can be the result of a failure to discern the Lord's body. He helps us see that healing and wholeness are directly linked to discernment, which explains why misinterpretations have triggered some of the very ailments that we attempt to pray away. Quoting Isaiah 53:5 is indeed beneficial in the wake of sickness, but applying First Corinthians 11 before it ever appears would be even more effective. Discernment, like communion, is a choice based on a revelation of the blood. It is a decision to ascend to a level of thought and response that reflects the existence that God planned for us, and a commitment to operate in that fullness. It is a decision to associate the supernatural with the Lord's body, while anticipating the miraculous in our own. Finally, it is a refusal to allow the enemy to wreak havoc in any area of our lives.

Let me explain it this way. One of the members of our church modeled discernment in a powerful way. Doctors said that her daughter, who could not walk or talk, would be "a vegetable" who would never lead a normal life. The mother rejected this report, prayed in faith, and consistently took communion as she waited for God to demonstrate in her daughter's life what is available at His Table. The Lord healed her daughter, who is now leading a normal life, enjoying her fourth year of school, and still reminding us that because Jesus bore illnesses in His body, we don't have to bear them in ours.

For if we would judge ourselves, we should not be judged.
– (1 Cor. 11:31)

Judgment, like the term blood, makes many of us uncomfortable because it is associated with sin. But sin is not the driving force behind judging ourselves; stewardship is. When we judge ourselves we take on Adam's assignment to tend the garden of our lives, quickly uprooting every weed that could obstruct the fruit of communion. We seek to reveal God's nature in thought, word, and deed by living a holy life; however, we do not depend on our strength alone to achieve this pursuit. We ask the Holy Spirit to examine our hearts and expose the sins of which we may not be aware. Sins like bitterness, resentment, unforgiveness, selfishness, and pride can choke our harvest of fellowship if they are allowed to run amuck, for when we harbor secret sins, they attract the very issues that Jesus overcame with His blood. Years of scientific research suggests that an individual can manifest hidden emotions physiologically, through conditions like back pain, high blood pressure, digestive issues, and chronic stress. The person's symptoms are treated, but because the cause (secret sin) goes unchecked, his body remains linked to a consequence of evil, illness. When we judge ourselves we expose and extract hidden sins, and we allow the supernatural work of communion to take place in our mind and in our body. In fact, Simply asking God to show us those we have wronged and those against whom we are holding a grudge could be the first step of relieving medical conditions!

When we make a resolution to judge ourselves so we are not judged, we also make sure that we are not judging others. When we hold sins and choose to judge others. we disregard Jesus' sacrifice by attempting to make people pay the penalty for sin, as if we were the Messiah. Judging ourselves means admitting our shortcomings and applying the blood of Jesus to them, but it also means forgiving others despite their faults. This means that judgment is not a punishment, but a tool that helps safeguard fellowship with God by maintaining the ground of our hearts. Walking in these revelations of judgment, discernment, and worthiness will give us the confidence to not only approach the Table, but also take a seat there.

So go ahead. Take your seat. Sit down knowing that you and the millions of believers on your left and right are only there because of the grace of God and the blood of Jesus. Sit down knowing that you were unworthy when you first accepted Jesus; that your sin didn't stop Him from saving you then and that it won't stop Him from communing with you now. Sit down knowing that no matter how good you have been, works can never make you worthy (1 Cor. 23:27). Sit down knowing that faith pulled out the chair for you, and that that seat will never fail you. Sit down knowing that you will eventually be called to stand up and go out to conduct God's business in the earth. And when you sit, expect the supernatural to manifest.

While you are sitting, you will be reminded of what the blood of Jesus accomplished for all of us. If you stay long enough, you'll meet the Syrophoenecian woman who hangs around the Table. She met Jesus a long time ago at a desperate point in her life. When she begged Him to heal her daughter from an evil spirit, He told her that healing was the children's bread, and that it was reserved for the people with whom He had covenant. But she told Him that even the dogs get the crumbs from the Master's Table. She was okay with getting the leftovers because she knew there was power in that meal. Jesus was so moved by her faith that He began to pull out chairs – one for her, one for her newly healed daughter, and millions more for the generations of Gentiles that would desire to come to His Table. The woman knew how to discern the body of Jesus and she lingers at the Table to help us make sure that no crumb, no moment of communion, gets wasted in unbelief.

If she's busy, you can talk to the guys from Emmaus. They met Jesus at a point of grief and utter despair. Jesus communed with them after the crucifixion, but the men did not know who He was until they partook of a covenant meal with Him. Then their eyes were opened and they realized why their hearts were ablaze. If you ever reach a place of pain or despair so intense that you can no longer recognize Jesus, they will help guide you back to the Table. It is the place that you will finally see Him as He is. When you see Him, you will be like Him, and you will be able to journey the path He traveled to reach the Table and to reach you.

PART II

Restoration through the Blood

One act of obedience is better than a hundred sermons.

- Deitrich Bonheoffer, Pastor, Theologian

CHAPTER 3

Gethsemane:
Redemption of the Will

The path is familiar to Him, but familiarity brings little comfort on a night like tonight. His feet have memorized the beaten paths between ancient olive trees in the garden called Gethsemane, and the moment demands that He traverse it alone. He commands us to keep watch with Him as He goes deeper into the Garden to pray, but the weight of sorrow resting on our eyelids compels us to commune with sleep instead of Him. While we are sleeping, our Pastor's soul is overcome with grief. Praying with such intensity that drops of blood form on His forehead, He asks for a way out - knowing that *He is the way*. He returns to find us asleep, and asks us to pray again. Though He is about to face an agonizing death, Jesus prompts us to pray for ourselves rather than Him. He knows that if we really commune with God in prayer, the Lord will share burdens of His heart with us and our petition will become intercession. Jesus goes back to the place of prayer and utters the same request as before. He comes again and finds us basking in the sea of numbness that sleep affords. The Son goes to His closet one more time, crucifying His own will as He walks through the door that leads to the Father's plan. He steps once more into our slumber and wakes us just in time to hear the alarm of a betrayer.

This place is called Gethsemane. A small olive orchard at the base of the Mount of Olives, its name combines two words to mean "oil press." Set between the mount and the Kidron brook, the site that King Asa burned and pulverized his mother's idol (2 Chron. 15:16), Gethsemane is the place of crushing. Here every plan that opposes prophetic destiny is trampled under foot, under *our* foot. In Gethsemane God's purpose for our lives is saluted with a *yes, Lord*, and His strength alone enables us to step into destiny, terrifying and lonely as it may feel. When we leave this sacred garden, we are never the same.

Before the foundation of the world was laid, God determined that the Garden of Gethsemane would be the first place that Jesus physically shed blood. Earlier we noted that blood sacrifices in the Old Testament were made in worship, in covenant, or for the propitiation of sin, with the latter pointing toward the perfect sacrifice that would accomplish God's purpose of redemption (Heb. 10:10-14). Every blood sacrifice for sin that preceded Jesus was used to withhold God's judgment as it related to a specific person or event, which allowed sins to be pardoned, but not exterminated from Adam's blood. Thus, believers of old awaited the promised Messiah who would die for their sins, for only His blood could address the issue of sin in humanity's bloodline. Just as they looked ahead, believers of today look back to the One whose blood signaled the culmination of God's promise.

GETHSEMANE: THE WILL

Shedding blood in specific areas to redeem particular elements of our being, Jesus first goes to a garden to deal with the human will (the soulish realm). More than any other place, the Garden of Gethsemane reveals the human will of Jesus, because in that place He is introduced to the depths of human experience that are rooted in Adam's bloodline. For the first time Jesus enters a wrestling match with Himself, humanity craving one thing and divinity pursuing another. His soul (will, mind, and emotions) is grieved to the point of death because His humanity is dying, and unlike the temptation in the wilderness, no one is coming to minister to Him. After facing triple disappointment from His beloved inner circle, The Word encounters a silent God who doesn't have to respond to petitions in the garden. That same silence seems to herald the ensuing absence of the Omnipresent One.

But the challenges didn't stop there. Not only was Jesus' will tested in Gethsemane; His body was, too. The way that Jesus shed blood in the garden can be understood as a medical condition called hematohidrosis. Also known as hematidrosis or hemidrosis, this rare condition occurs when the capillary blood vessels feeding sweat glands rupture, causing them to secrete blood. Most cases of hematohidrosis are triggered by severe anxiety and intense mental contemplation, and they typically happen when a person experiences states of tremendous physical and/or emotional stress. Blood vessels around the sweat glands constrict under the pressure of stress, and as the anxiety increases, the vessels expand to the point of rupture. Blood goes into the sweat glands, pushing it, along with sweat, to the skin's surface. The severe mental anxiety prompts the sympathetic nervous system to invoke the 'fight or flight' reaction to such a degree that vessels hemorrhage. Most people who have suffered from this condition feel extremely weak after such severe episodes. If Jesus experienced hematohidrosis while in Gethsemane, it would have been His first personal exposure to a physical condition. No Scriptural passage asserts or even alludes to Him being plagued by any type of illness prior to this moment, so it seems that the consequences of Adam's blood start to effect Jesus' body before He ever leaves the garden.

Blood is Thicker than Water

Gethsemane reminds us that bloodlines carry a blessing or a curse (Lk. 22:44). Because sweat is the physical reminder that Adam's sin led to God cursing the ground, when Jesus sweats a mixture of perspiration and blood (representing His humanity and divinity), He overcomes the curse in Adam's bloodline by shedding drops of sinless blood. In so doing, Jesus applies His blood to the human will and mind. The blood on Jesus' head acts as a cleansing agent for every curse in the mind or will of man. It reforms what has been distorted in the soul and allows us to replace the human will with God's will. Just as drops of blood were sprinkled on the altar (representing God's presence) in the Old Testament (Lev. 4:6; 4:17; 5:9), so were drops of blood sprinkled on the ground (representing man's presence) in the New.

The blood of Jesus strategically parallels contexts found in the Old Testament to bring us back into God's intent for humanity. Hence, Jesus reestablishes in Gethsemane what Adam lost in Eden, because the last Adam never gives in to temptation. He sheds His blood to cover the sins of humanity like God shed an animal's blood to cover the sins of Adam and Eve. This blood overcomes the curse of sin with the blessing of redemption and gives us authority over the human will.

The human will is indelibly linked to Adam's blood, while God's will is directly connected to the blood of Jesus. When Jesus denies His own will in the Garden of Gethsemane, He simultaneously rejects and conquers Adam's blood. The effects of Adam's blood are most potent in the mind, though they are often manifested in the body, which is inclined to sin and bent toward every negative consequence of evil. Transferred to future generations when left unchecked, these consequences try to contest the blood of Jesus by justifying recurring sin and vicious cycles in the lineage. We notice it when people anticipate and excuse sin just because 'it runs in the family.' While we are not ignorant of generational curses, because of the blood of Jesus, we are also not bound to them. Failure to break the curse is a blatant disregard of that blood, which was shed that our will might be made one with the Father's.

Anytime the Lord leads us into a Gethsemane (a place of crushing), His agenda is to align our will and mind with His eternal purpose. That alignment comes as we apply the blood of Jesus to our will, and deal with the blood that carries an opposing will. Scripture teaches us that the blood type determines the mindset, or disposition of the heart. Exodus 14:5 says, "When the king of Egypt was told that the people had fled, the mind of Pharaoh and his servants was changed toward the people, and they said, 'What is this we have done, that we have let Israel go from serving us?'" Some translations of this passage say that Pharaoh's heart (meaning inner man, will, mind) was changed. The heart is indicative of the mind in both physical and spiritual ways. Physically speaking, the heart's intrinsic nervous system is so complex and sophisticated that it qualifies as a small brain. In fact, it houses proteins, neurons, neurotransmitters, and support cells that are similar to the ones found in the human brain. In addition to processing and transmitting detailed information, the heart also sends blood to the body. Knowing how the heart interacts with the brain helps shape our understanding of God's spiritual dealings with the mind. We noted earlier that the human will is indicative of Adam's blood, and since the heart *processes* and transmits information through the blood, we can deduce that the blood type influences our reaction to that information. Said another way, the type of blood, be it pure or poisoned, is revealed through our response to the information given us. Therefore, when God changes the heart or mind, He not only adjusts the ways that we process information, but also ways that we apply it.

The Lord transforms the heart and mind to mentally position us for His purpose and His promise. Satan, on the other hand, works to imprison us with a flawed mindset, because he knows that it can keep us from walking in dominion. This is exactly what happened to the first generation of Israelites, whose tribal leaders spied out the land of Canaan. Barring Joshua and Caleb, every leader confessed an evil report:

> *The land, through which we have gone to search it, is a land that eats up the inhabitants thereof; and all the people that we saw in it are men of a great stature. And there we saw the giants, […] and we were in our own sight as grasshoppers, and so we were in their sight*
> – (Num. 13:32a-33)

Because these leaders still held an Adamic mentality, they caused an entire generation to forfeit God's promise. God's invitation to the Promised Land was a summons into supernatural living that would reflect Eden before the fall of man. The Lord had already supplied miraculous provision for Israel to access and fully possess this land, but Adam's mindset caused them to fear the very thing that belonged to them. When fear entered, it completely warped the leaders' perception of themselves.

The tribal rulers were so bound by Adam's mindset that they declared and accepted an even lower state of being than that which was given to humankind; they likened themselves to insects. Mere pests in their own eyes (Hebrew *ayin*, meaning organs, mental qualities, or spiritual faculties), the spies could not embrace their God-given status or the mindset that would undergird it. Instead, they remembered the plagues in Egypt and took on a mentality consistent with that of a grasshopper, one species of which is the locust. Swarming locusts change their behavior, are accustomed to migration rather than settlement, and focus only on self-preservation. In the same manner, the first generation of Israelites changed behavior shortly after being delivered; preferred migration over settling in the Promised Land; and sought preservation rather than manifestation. The mindset of the locust consumed in Israel's heart what the insect itself devoured in Egypt's fields – rich resources that would bring communal prosperity. When the locust mentality infected the perception and confession of Israel's leaders, the entire nation lowered its standard of existence. Their distorted perception became reality, because as a man thinks, so is he (Prov. 23:7).

The contaminants in Adam's blood blurred the vision of these leaders, making it difficult to see themselves as God did and to know that He was still with them. The rulers had witnessed God's presence in spectacular wonders in Egypt, and observed Him through fire, smoke, and clouds in the wilderness, but they did not know how to trace God without these exhibitions. Their ignorance stirred a viewpoint of stark separation instead of covenantal communion, and that made it much easier to embrace the human will and reject the divine will. Soon God's chosen people began to frame their world with words of panic and not of promise. Since every word is the product of a thought, and every thought reveals what is in the blood, their negative decrees signaled double contamination—a tainted bloodline and a polluted mind. As a result, millions of Israelites lived and died much like grasshoppers; with daily provision but without any sense of divine purpose.

Purpose is connected to and realized through the mind of Christ. To take on His mind we must go beyond the altar and back to Eden, where we first see God's intention for the human mind and will. Before sin entered the world God communed with Adam uninterruptedly, walking and talking with the man who looked just like his Father. But when Adam chose to sin, he interrupted communion and created a blood sport of the mind that would affect every generation. This birthed a competition of the wills that could be won only by the man named Jesus.

The blood of Jesus restores us back to God's original intent, renews our willpower, brings salvation to our minds, and severs every mental and psychological stronghold by bringing reformation to our whole being. We are three-part beings made up of spirit (pneuma), soul (psyche), and body (soma). Our spirit is wired to say yes to God, and that yes penetrates the soul (will, mind, emotions) to manifest through deeds of the body. The blood allows us to fulfill God's will with our entire being, because it gives us power over the human will.

When we apply the blood, we receive supernatural assistance to obey and execute the will of God as our own will is cleansed and sanctified. Only through the blood can we address and overcome issues common to Adam. As we appropriate the blood of Jesus and disable the issues that seek to destroy our generation, we realize that God doesn't just lead us to Gethsemane to crush the human will; He also leads us there that we might crush the serpents head (brain center, sinful mindset). When we use the blood to crush the mentality that would keep us in bondage, the Lord changes our perception of Gethsemane from a site of loss to a place of victory. We maintain the victory by consistently applying the blood and by engaging the mind of Christ, which enables us to operate in creative power.

It's All in Your Mind

The mind of Christ is the creative realm of thinking (communicating) that reveals God's nature and mission. By studying the recorded thoughts of God through the Holy Spirit, we are able to understand more of His nature and purpose for our lives. We first see the mind of Christ in Genesis 1, when the persons of the Trinity converse (think) about making humanity. Their conversation is held in the unity of the Spirit and it reveals God's intention for dominion in earth (Eph. 4:3). When Jesus became flesh, He literally made this realm of thinking tangible. His mind is a supernatural state of thought that manifests God's will and purpose. To search the it is to explore the seven-fold Spirit of God, which is spoken of by the prophet Isaiah. He declares,

"And there shall come forth a rod out of the stem of Jesse, and a Branch shall grow out of his roots: And the spirit of the LORD shall rest upon him, the spirit of wisdom and understanding, the spirit of counsel and might, the spirit of knowledge and of the fear of the LORD (Isa. 11:1-2)."

We will briefly discuss each of these spirits, but will give most attention to the Spirit of the Lord, which envelops all others listed here. The Spirit of the Lord is the supernatural source of power that generates God's thoughts in our hearts and minds; the Spirit of wisdom encompasses the thoughts themselves; the Spirit of understanding is God's personal illumination of these thoughts so humans may know how to apply them; the Spirit of counsel is God's personal instruction for particular situations; the Spirit of strength is the ability to implement that instruction in the personal life of the believer; the Spirit of knowledge is the manifestation of God's thoughts in the believer's actions; and the Fear of the Lord is the capacity to operate reverently before God by walking in truth and love, and resisting anything that would quench His spirit.

The Spirit of the Lord, which is to say, the Holy Spirit, is not only the force behind God's thoughts that makes it possible for other facets of God to permeate our lives, but also the divine person of the Trinity who empowers us to perform these thoughts for the glory of God. In other words, we possess the mind of Christ through the Holy Spirit, who is identical in nature to the Father and the Son. When the Holy Spirit enters a believer's heart, He begins to transition their thought-life by leading the individual towards the mind of Christ, and by teaching and reminding that person of God's word (Jn. 14:26). He moves in God's people to bring about comprehensive mental overhaul by working with us, dwelling in us, coming upon us, and continually refilling us.

Before we confess Jesus as Lord, the Holy Spirit works *with* us to guide us to Christ. He convicts us of sin and shows us that Jesus is the way out of it. The moment we are saved, the Holy Spirit comes to dwell *in* us, causing the Spirit of God to become the indwelling power source of our lives (Rom. 8:9). At some point, the Spirit of God comes *upon* us to enlighten, embolden, and empower us, as we see in Acts 2 when the Holy Spirit comes upon the disciples that they may receive power to become witnesses. Once the Spirit of the Lord has come upon us, He constantly refills us with His Spirit. This is what Paul points to in Romans 12:2 when he commands believers, "be not conformed to this world: but be ye transformed by the renewing of your mind, that ye may prove what is that good, and acceptable, and perfect, will of God." The seven fold Spirit of God equips us to prove (distinguish) the *will* of God, but we must engage His Spirit to rightly discern His will from the human will. We sharpen the ability to discern by continuously renewing our mind.

We renew the mind by reading and hearing the Word of God; by praying without ceasing; by practicing spiritual disciplines (such as fasting) that intentionally kill the flesh; by partaking of daily communion; by fellowshipping with like-minded believers; by confessing decrees based on the Word; and by submitting to the spiritual leaders to whom God has called us. A renewed mind allows the mind of Christ to saturate our operation in the realm of the Spirit. As the Lord transforms (reforms) us back to His original design, we activate and cultivate a supernatural mind.

When we allow the mind of Christ to exist and operate in us (Phil. 2:5), we structure our lives around the Genesis mandate. A renewed mind establishes the communication of heaven in us until our very thoughts manifest dominion in the earth. One sign of that dominion is the ability to bring into captivity every thought to the obedience of Christ (2 Cor. 10:5). Taking every thought captive also protects the mind from self-sabotage and mental breakdown. A scene from the film *The Great Debaters* might help illustrate this principle.

In the film, Denzel Washington plays a nonconformist professor who educates students in history and the skills of rhetoric. When one daring student sharply retorts at him, Washington notes Willie Lynch's instruction to take the mind of slaves, and offers, "I, and every other professor on this campus, are here to help you to find, take back, and keep your righteous mind; because obviously you have lost it." Just as Washington's character teaches students to protect the mind by cultivating it, so the Holy Spirit teaches us how to guard our mind by renewing it. This shields us from mental dis-integration, the literal loss of integrity in the mind.

As we put away any opposing will, we nourish fruits of the Spirit that reveal God's nature. This practice helps us to choose God's will until it becomes our preference, a transition that indicates a refilling of the Holy Spirit. When the heart and mind are aligned with God's will, we become filled with the fullness of God (Eph. 3:19).

A renewed mind allows us to glean from Gethsemane, because we begin to understand that the blood shed gives us access to Eden. The drops of blood on Jesus' head have redeemed our will and restored our mind. Pounding the ground one by one, they form a scarlet stream that flows from our spirit into our soul, enabling us to commune with God in the very place that we once deserted Him-- the mind.

I, Jehovah, am healing thee.

Exodus 15:26 (YLT)

CHAPTER 4

The Whipping Post:
Restoration of Physical Healing

Look away. It's much easier to do so than it is to watch the soldier clasp that cat of nine tails. The awful lash bears nine smaller whips that hold jagged pieces of rock and metal destined for Jesus' body. We wonder, with eyes covered, why the law allows soldiers to beat prisoners before crucifixion, knowing that those who manage to survive the beating are in a physical state of shock when they finally meet the cross. The sound of jingling metal interrupts our thoughts and grabs our attention just in time to see the wounded Healer's body ripped open. The lash breaks His flesh thirty nine times; one for every book of the Old Covenant and for every root cause of disease. Eyes wide shut, we see the brutality in high definition. And yet, seeing this image of Jesus still doesn't give us a revelation of who He is. Since we can't esteem the One we don't understand, we hide our faces again.

We've become experts at hiding. Adam taught us well. Hiding keeps us from seeing that Jesus bears our griefs and sorrows, and takes on every offensive element for a people who deem Him stricken and smitten. Faces concealed, eyes clinched, heart pounding, we wait for the jingling to finally cease. The quiet commands us to open our eyes. Slowly, we lift the veils. Blood is everywhere, as are chunks of flesh now soaked in a liquid cloak. The sight is horrid. So disfigured is the Word's frame that His body no longer resembles humanity. Wait. Maybe it does. Maybe it displays exactly what sin has done to us; a marring so penetrating that those created in God's image now look nothing like their Father. Only the stream flowing from Jesus' stripes can restore that image while sealing an ancient covenant and healing every disease.

The Covenant-Keeping God

The merciless beating at the whipping post was the very channel that God used to ratify His covenant with Abraham and to procure healing for his seed. This covenant, which is known in Hebrew as *berit*, was a sacred agreement that confirmed God's initiative to bind Himself to Abraham, a mere man. History contains many records of kings of this era who bestowed gifts to subjects without receiving one in return, so we know that royal endowments or agreements were common in Abraham's day. These unwarranted grants were issued under the king's seal, and sometimes under his oath, just as we see in God's oath to Abraham.

Abraham made all of the standard preparations to make ready for the covenant ceremony with God (Gen. 15:9-18). He divided animals in two and arranged their parts for the formal swearing, an act that would traditionally accompany an oath similar to this one:

"As this animal is torn in two, so may I be if I sever this covenant." The tearing of flesh is arguably the most important part of the ceremony, for it combines shed blood and the word.

Abraham shed the blood of animals during the covenant ritual and eventually shed his own blood because of circumcision, but because God Himself never shed blood during these covenantal rites, the agreements remained unratified. Since Jesus was God in flesh, His blood was that of God Himself. Thus, when Jesus shed blood during His suffering and death, God's blood was shed, and that blood alone was able to ratify the covenant made with Abraham.

Symbolically shed during the Lord's Supper, blood pours from Jesus' body like wine at the whipping post, which caused communion to become a substitute feast for the blood covenant of friendship. The blood covenant of friendship was an ancient agreements that included a feast in which two partners would eat the flesh and drink the blood (wine or juice) of an animal substitute that represented the life of each partner. In so doing, a partner would, as it were, take into himself the very life of the other; such that each person held his own life in addition to that of the partner. In like manner, when we partake of the Lord's Supper, we take into ourselves the substitute for God's body and blood, which links our lives to His. God's life is in us through the Holy Spirit, who makes real in us what Jesus completed for believers through His life, death, and resurrection; namely salvation for the soul and healing for the body (1 Jn. 1:7). By recognizing the significance of meals that indicate a blood covenant of friendship, we find parallels that increase our revelation of communion. Let's begin by discussing one meal of that sort, Passover, which accomplished for Israel what Jesus achieved for humanity.

In preparation for Passover, God instructs Moses to command Israelite households to kill a lamb and place its blood on their doorposts. Every Israelite household is to eat the same meal: lamb, unleavened bread, and bitter herbs. The meal is to be consumed hastily, and those eating are to have loins girded, feet shod, and staffs in hand so as to make ready for a swift departure from Egypt (Ex. 12:2-11). Like the Lord's Supper, this natural meal has supernatural qualities. As the Israelites consumed this miraculous meal, they were healed of every infirmity that could hinder an escape from bondage, and were strengthened to complete such an arduous journey. Scholars estimate that two to three million Israelites (600,000 men plus women and children) left Egypt, and Psalm 105:37 tells us that none of them were feeble (sick). This means that not a single person was afflicted with diabetes or sickle cell, a headache or a sinus infection, a lethal virus or a skin disease, because every individual partook of the meal. Just imagine if such a thing happened today! What if another group of about three million people, like the population of the state of Arkansas, was totally free of illness for a period of time? What if emergency rooms were empty and every hospital room was vacant? What if urgent care clinics were bare and pharmacies were deserted? What if we stopped hiding our faces and covering our eyes and finally saw what the suffering, death, and resurrection of Jesus has provided for us?

We would see Psalm 103 in our lives and not just our Bibles. Looking closely at the first three verses of this chapter will help us appreciate the supernatural effects of communion. The psalmist commands, "Bless the LORD, O my soul: and all that is within me, bless his holy name. Bless the LORD, O my soul, and forget not all his benefits: Who forgives all your iniquities; who heals all your diseases."

THE WHIPPING POST: PHYSICAL HEALING

The psalmist connects blessing the Lord to remembering Him, and this connection is indicative of communion. When everything in us receives a command to bless the Lord, every physical component of our body and every element in the bloodline of our natural father must completely align with His spirit. A lifestyle of communion fosters our inclination to bless the Lord, and keeps us mindful of the blood covenant that God made with Abraham and ratified through Jesus. The terms of this ratified covenant nullify the power of sickness, so we refuse to allow any physical ailment or emotional condition (e.g. depression, isolation, etc.) to have power over our body or mind. No harmful condition has the right to come near us because the blood covenant makes us one with God. As He is, so are we.

Since disease has no power over God, it also has no power over us. We have learned not to strengthen sickness with our words, so we do not claim it for ourselves or confess its ability to cause death. Disease was stripped of all authority at the whipping post so it cannot demand the life of a person. God may allow an individual to transition from this life to the next while the body is afflicted, but no one dies *from* cancer or hepatitis or any other disease. This type of language is a subtle trick that the enemy uses to bolster the presence and activity of illness in our bloodline, because negative words give him access to us. If we have given verbal credence to sickness, we must seal all openings by pleading the blood of Jesus and applying His healing to every generation of our predecessors and descendants. We also partake of communion and confess the Word. Communion removes false notions from the mind while the blood cancels issues in our bloodline, for full manifestations of deliverance occur only when the bloodline is cleansed. We also train our children to guard their confessions and views of illness by emphasizing the power of the blood over every disease. As we and those in our generation employ words to reiterate the blood, we position ourselves to access all of God's benefits.

The benefits of God include 60 covenant promises that He gave to Abraham and his descendants in an agreement that made provision for generations. The generational blessing suggests that God never has just one person in mind, and the Bible shows us that those who consistently commune with Him also model this attribute. Remember Mephibosheth? He was the son of Jonathan, David's close friend. David promised to bless Jonathan's house as long as David lived, and he kept this vow long after Jonathan died. When he learned that Mephibosheth was living far beneath his privileges in Lo Debar, a place that literally means pastureless, the former shepherd called Jonathan's son into the palace and promised to forever nourish him and his entire house. Though he was not David's son or relative, Mephibosheth was the seed of a man with whom a covenant was made. As a result, he and all connected to him enjoyed security and prosperity for the rest of their lives. If David, a mere man operating under an old covenant, could make provision for many lives based on an agreement with another human, how much more has God provided for us under the new covenant? We have a better covenant than the one to which David had access, because we have the blood of Jesus.

The blood seals us for healing and provides all things that we need for life and godliness, or God-likeness (Heb. 6:8; 11:40; 1 Pet. 1:3). These things all point toward the five-fold ministry (the apostolic, prophetic, evangelistic, pastoral, and didactic [teacher] callings), and to the gifts of the supernatural: wisdom, knowledge, faith, healing, miracles, prophecy, discernment, languages, and interpretation (Eph.

4:11-13; 1 Cor. 12:7-11). The benefits that we receive from the ratified blood covenant ensure the security and prosperity, salvation and healing, gifts and callings necessary to fully walk in and demonstrate our God-likeness.

But benefits are useless if they remain un-accessed. The family of Henrietta Lacks knows this all too well. Henrietta Lacks was a poor African American woman whose cells impacted the field of science and medicine in immeasurable ways. Taken without her knowledge during a hospital visit in 1951, the cells were kept alive and multiplied, and ultimately utilized to start a cell line that would be used for research in medicine, polio vaccination, gene mapping, in-vitro fertilization, cancer research, and a host of other scientific discoveries. What's striking about these cells is that they came from a woman with poisoned blood. Mrs. Lacks died of uremic poisoning, a condition that develops from excessive waste in the bloodstream. Despite the poisoned blood, Mrs. Lacks' cells are thriving over 60 years later and continuing to help heal countless numbers of people. Yet, these cells are but a shadow of what Jesus' blood has done for us. His blood can never die, and it secures both natural and spiritual life for those who apply it. Because Mrs. Lacks' family was unaware of her procedure and the benefits of her cells, they did not receive the wealth accrued from the cells' utilization. Many of her family members have struggled so much financially that they cannot afford the very health insurance that enables strangers to profit from the cells in their lineage. While we do not blame her family for a lack of knowledge, their experience does teach us that when we, the descendants of the Healer, fail to access the covenant's benefits, we restrict healing and wholeness from every part of our lives, and, like Mephibosheth, live far beneath our privileges.

The blood of Jesus provides healing for the whole person (spirit, soul, and body), so we have a kingdom right and obligation to enforce healing in our lives. The Lord has given us the resources and the authority to do so. Each time we take communion, we partake of that healing and appropriate the benefits of the blood covenant. Like the kings of Israel in days of old, we are each held responsible for aligning with and manifesting the statutes of God; one of which is healing for our bloodline (Matt. 10:1; Lk. 5:17). People who believe that physical healing was restricted to Jesus' day, or that God cares for the spirit alone and has no dealings with the rest of the person cannot fulfill this responsibility. Both of these notions are grave errors that call our attention to the gift of healing in Scripture. After studying healing in the Old and New Testament, we will better understand God's personal healing work, His healing work through people and through the Church, and His methods of healing. This will help teach us how to walk in supernatural healing in every area of our lives.

The Lord as Healer

The Bible contains many demonstrations of God as Healer (Jehovah Rapha). We just discussed how His covenant with Abraham secured healing for many generations, and noted how He used a meal to heal the Israelites before they left Egypt. God also healed the barren wombs of Sarah, Rachel, and Hannah (Gen. 21:1-2; Gen. 30:22; 1 Sam. 1:19-20). His pattern established a precedent of healing that would mark Jesus' ministry. The prophet Isaiah proclaimed a word about this to Israel, "Your God will come, [...] Then will the eyes of the blind be opened and the ears of the deaf unstopped. Then will the lame leap like a deer, and the mute tongue shout for joy (Isa. 35:4b-6a)." Jesus fulfills this prophecy in entirety with many instances of direct healing throughout His ministry. We find three specific examples of healing in a single passage, Matthew 9:18-31, which chronicles the resurrection of the ruler's daughter, the restoration of the woman with the issue of blood, and the healing of the blind men. Matthew 4:23-24 gives a more general account of Jesus (God) as Healer:

"Jesus went throughout Galilee [...] healing every disease and sickness among the people. News about him spread all over Syria, and people brought to him all who were ill with various diseases, those suffering severe pain, the demon-possessed, those having seizures, and the paralyzed, and he healed them."

Jesus' response to John's disciples in Luke 7:20-22 echoes the claim that Matthew recorded:

"When the men came to Jesus, they said, "John the Baptist sent us to you to ask, 'Are you the one, or shall we look for another?' At that very time Jesus cured many who had diseases, sicknesses and evil spirits, and gave sight to many who were blind. So he replied to the messengers, "Go back and report to John what you have seen and heard: The blind receive sight, the lame walk, those who have leprosy are cured, the deaf hear, the dead are raised, and the good news is preached to the poor."

Jesus not only heals the masses, but also those who bear the fruits of damnation: the weak, (Peter's mother-in-law), the sick (the ten lepers), and those who sleep, or die prematurely (Lazarus). Jesus employs the same gift of healing in the New Testament that God exhibits in the Old, and thereby reveals that miraculous demonstrations of healing are common to His ministry and to the supernatural.

Jesus understands that Adam's sin is the origin of sickness, and knows that His blood is the cure. So while He is acquainted with sickness and disease through those He heals, His suffering at the whipping post would become the single greatest demonstration of God as healer. His blood heals His *own* body, even as it provides healing for ours.

God Working Through People

God's Word is full of stories that tell of His healing work through people. To comprehend this work we must learn how healing was viewed in the Old and New Testaments. In the Old Testament, the Hebrew word *rapha* is used more than any other term for healing, and it means "to mend by stitching" or "to cure." The word denotes restoration for individuals and nations (2 Chron. 7:14); curing (Isa. 19:22); forgiveness (Hos. 14:4); comfort (Job 13:4); making whole (2 Kgs. 2:21-22); and healing through repentance (Hos. 6:1). In the Old Testament God acts as a master surgeon who sometimes operates alone, but often uses people to help bind up the broken. The Lord uses Abraham to usher in healing for Abimelech, his wife, and his servants (Gen. 20:17-18), while Moses intercedes for Miriam's healing from leprosy (Ex. 4:6-7, 30). Elisha, who walked in the spirit of communion, brings back to life the son of a Shunnamite woman who was once barren, ushering healing in her house first through conception and then through resurrection (2 Kgs. 4:33-37). The same prophet facilitates Naaman's healing from leprosy (2 Kgs. 5:1-19). These occurrences all reflect the Old Testament's depiction of healing as a restorative agent.

Healing is also an integral part of New Testament church life, and it carries a different shade of meaning than we see in the Old Testament. The word used most often for healing in the New Testament is *therapeuo*, the Greek term from which we get therapy.

THE WHIPPING POST: PHYSICAL HEALING

This term comes from a word that means attendant or servant, and it also means to wait upon menially, to adore (God) or to relieve (of illness). Demonstrations of this description are throughout the New Testament. Relief comes when Paul heals the father of Publius (Acts 26:7-10), when he restores a crippled man (Acts 14:8-10), when Peter heals a lame beggar (Acts 3:1-9) and when his shadow heals multitudes (Acts 5:12-16). Since the term therapeuo expresses an ability to cure, heal, or worship, several manifestations of healing in the New Testament combine these descriptions. For example, the father of a demon-possessed boy worships Jesus and then his son is healed/delivered (Matt. 17:14-18); Jesus resurrects a dead boy and all who witness this healing begin to adore God (Luke 7:13-16); the mother of a demon-possessed daughter worships Jesus and her child is delivered (Mk. 7:24-30); Jesus heals a woman of an infirmity lasting eighteen years while ministering to (serving) people in the temple, and she leaves glorifying God (Lk. 13:10-13); and Paul resurrects a dead man who falls out of a window during a worship gathering (Acts 20:7-12). We notice that healing in the New Testament is frequently linked to service (be it to God or man), and that the approach to healing seems more proactive here than in the Old Testament, where healing typically comes after a request is made. Although Jesus does respond to requests for healing, He is much more intentional about seeking (attending to, waiting on) those who need to be made whole. His decisions to heal people who do not make a request, like the paralytic at Bethesda, the man with a disfigured hand, and the demon-possessed man among the tombs all evidence this intentionality. His approach to the ministry of healing institutes a new paradigm of restoration that makes no accommodation for sickness.

In the same manner, we must actively seek healing, because

it is our portion. However, we do recognize that some illnesses, like that of the blind child in Scripture, are permitted so the glory of God can be revealed in a generation (Jn. 9:2-3). At times the Lord allows sickness to manifest in our lives because He wants us to bring reformation to our bloodline. He will reveal generational issues to sons and daughters whom He trusts to break the cycle. Healing is already sealed in our spirit, but it must reach the mind and body (the two elements that expose what is in the bloodline), and that kind of transfer only happens when we work with God. We reach the mind by studying and confessing the word of God, and the body by following the laws of health that God has outlined for us. We also search our heart to ensure that no offense or unforgiveness has created an emotional wound that could become an access point for physical affliction.

Almost every hindrance to healing is subtle, so we need to be mindful of the attitudes, practices, and responses that can connect us to illness. Some of the things that can impede healing are: sin (Isa. 59:2, Matt. 13:15), unbelief (Matt. 13:58, Mk. 6:5), the abuse of our bodies (1 Cor. 3:16-17; Phil. 2:25-30), and not discerning the Lord's body at His Table (I Cor. 11:29-33). Strained marital relationships (1 Pet. 3:1-7) and demonic resistance (Dan. 10:12-13) can also block healing from flowing in our bloodline. Therefore, we keep vigilant watch over the mind and body, especially during sickness, while we continue to apply the blood of Jesus to our lives and to future generations.

How God Heals

God's healing power is bestowed on some of His servants through the gift of healing, which is the God-given ability to impart healing to the physical body at specific times for the sake of advancing the kingdom. Though we may not all have the gift of healing (for we each have different gifts), grasping the nature of this gift can greatly impact our entire bloodline. At the same time that Jesus gave the apostles, along with seventy other disciples, the power to heal the sick, He gave instruction to preach the gospel (Lk. 7:21; 9:1-6; 10:1-9). He did so because the two are closely connected. Where the gospel is preached, healing of some sort (physical, emotional, or spiritual) takes place, since the gift of healing is one of the manifestations of the Holy Spirit. Like all spiritual gifts, the gift of healing points our attention back to God's character, and to the communion that Jesus' blood made possible.

The Lord uses doctors and medical science to display what the blood has already accomplished, but when we reference the gift of healing we speak of restoration of the infirmed without any scientific means. Some of us have seen the gift of healing at work and have noticed that it often accompanies a measure of the gift of faith and a word of knowledge, particularly when a person with the gift imparts faith to the one needing to be healed in order to lift him from the realm of doubt and unbelief. But this gift is only one method that God uses to bring healing. The Bible teaches us that healing can come through: the laying on of hands (Mk. 16:16-18); the spoken word (Matt. 8:5-13); elders in the local church (Jas. 5:14); the prayer of faith (James 5:15); the Lord's Supper (1 Cor. 11:23-34); a point of contact (Mk. 6:56); anointed cloths (Acts 19:11-12); and casting out devils (Lk. 8:26-39). It can also operate through tangible resources, like the figs that Isaiah uses in Hezekiah's healing (2 Kgs. 20:1-7); the saliva that Jesus uses to heal the blind man (John 9:6-7); the oil that the apostles use to heal the sick (Mk. 6:7-13); and the wine that Paul instructs Timothy to take for a stomach illness (1 Tim. 5:23). Many people doubt the gift of healing because they do not understand that it can operate on more than one level. For example, some healings are conditional (2 Kgs. 5:1-9) and others are not (Matt. 20:29-34). Some are gradual (Mk. 8:22-5) and others are instantaneous (Matt. 8:3). Variations of healing can indicate different levels of faith and method, but they are all made possible through the blood.

Faith in Jesus' redemptive sacrifice allows us to view the blood through God's eternal purpose and not through our own sin. It establishes our understanding of God's ultimate plan, and enables us to set present circumstances against a background of greater revelation. When this happens, we finally start to uncover our eyes.

Slowly, but surely, we see how the blood at the whipping post obtained our healing and our salvation, while ratifying an ancient covenant. Empowered to look on our King in the natural, and like Him in the spirit, we summon every ounce of strength to set our eyes on the journey ahead.

Untilled ground, however rich, will bring forth thistles and thorns; so also the mind of man.

- Teresa of Avila, 16th Century Saint

CHAPTER 5

The Crown of Thorns:
Restoration of Wealth

It's too late to turn back now. His back is sliced open and we can't even distinguish His frame, but He must finish the work. Peter's failed attempt to save the Savior from this moment enters our thoughts, creeping past the love and terror waiting at the door. Our eyes ask why to no avail as we glance at Him and look back at one another. These glimpses must be kept short, lest someone gain the courage to utter the other question hanging in the air like mistletoe… "If this is happening to Jesus, what will happen to us?" Afraid to know the answer, we guise the desperate expressions painting our faces and follow the trail of blood stemming from the whipping post.

We expect the soldiers to take Jesus to the place of crucifixion, but the pseudo-shepherds deviate from that path. They lead the Lamb to a hall and surround Him like wolves, beating His body with hands and assaulting His heart with empty worship. They cloak His shoulders in a robe of mockery. We flinch at how heavy that counterfeit mantle must be. After they taunt and batter Him with a fake scepter, the soldiers shape thorny branches into a circle of cruelty. Please, God. Please make them stop. They continue despite our blinded prayers, mashing wooden syringes into Jesus' scalp to ensure that His crown stays in place. Blood rushes to the surface of His head, and follows the contours of His face and neck to create new paths of deliverance. Lashes matted with coats of blood, the King sees past His own pain to secure our prosperity.

Every place that Jesus shed blood ushers in the blessing of God and purges out the curse of sin. The crown of thorns punctures Jesus flesh in several places, and these openings represent spiritual portals in the mind through which wealth can be channeled. Said another way, Jesus' head is penetrated with thorns so our minds can be penetrated with wealth. His shed blood triggers a divine exchange that not only restores the prosperity of Eden, but also releases the mindset of kingdom wealth needed to manifest that garden today.

Kingdom wealth is inextricably linked to faith, and it is only transferred to and facilitated through believers free of poverty. Poverty, like wealth, is a mindset. Many associate poverty with drastic insufficiency, but it is actually a spiritual manner of thinking and existing that is marked by an inability to create. The impoverished mindset comes from Satan, who cannot create, though he can pervert and utilize that which has been created. This is why he used what already existed (fruit) to tempt Eve, rather than creating something new. But make no mistake; an inability to create does not mean that Satan and his kingdom are without resources. His kingdom gains resources, in part, by increasing the influence of poverty in the Church and the world. When God's people are blinded, not having their minds enlightened by the truth of His word, they become vulnerable to impoverished thinking. Though believers still have the ability to create because we are made in God's image, the presence of poverty brings about an intense struggle to generate new ideas, concepts, strategies and inventions that bring wealth. Without new creations and a mind to manage those already present, the spirit of lack gains a foothold and begins to manifest drastic insufficiency. While believers combat natural and spiritual destitution, the enemy accesses the storehouse of their thought-life, which is the creation center designed to yield riches and wealth for God's kingdom. He knows that when poverty inhabits and ransacks this center, it takes on morbid attributes that ultimately strip the believer and strengthen the kingdom of darkness.

Poverty has four basic characteristics: It is never satisfied; it always seeks attention and glory; it opposes God's order; and it always appeals to flesh. Solomon teaches:

"There are three things that are never satisfied, yea, four things say not, It is enough: The grave (death); and the barren womb (absence of new life); the earth that is not filled with water (drought; man without the Holy Spirit); and the fire (Hell) (Prov. 30:15b-16)."

These four entities are voracious consumers, but like poverty, they all depend on a form of absence to exist, and they all lack the power to create. The second characteristic of poverty is its quest for attention and glory. Desperate for recognition because it is unworthy of association with God's greatest creation (humanity), the spirit of poverty always seeks exaltation to compensate for its lack of worth. No one demonstrates this trait better than Lucifer, who tried to usurp God's glory (Isa. 4:4-17). Poverty also opposes God's order. It hoards and controls resources in fear because it cannot properly steward them. We see this trait in the Pharaoh who knew not Joseph, when he convinced Egypt to enslave the Israelites for fear of them multiplying and overpowering the Egyptians (Ex. 8:9-11). Unable to apply a mindset of kingdom wealth, the Pharaoh stifled the order of prosperity by imposing bondage, and thus demonstrated the fourth trait of poverty - an appeal to and dependence on the flesh. Without fail, the spirit of poverty presents a carnal method to fulfill a spiritual need, because it can only utilize what it can manipulate. We see this characteristic in Lot's daughters, who get their father drunk so they can lie with him to preserve his name (Gen. 19:30-38). Acting out of an impoverished mindset, the two women appeal to Lot's flesh and depend on their own to accomplish God's command to be fruitful. They show us that the strength of poverty lies in a carnal mindset, the very place that thorns and thistles grow (Matt. 13:22).

Thorns and thistles are mental barriers that hinder the ability to produce. They accompany poverty because it guarantees a lack of production. We first witness this collaboration in Eden after the fall of man. While hiding among the trees of the garden Adam admits, "I heard Your voice in the garden, and I was afraid because I was naked (Gen. 3:10)." Though always naked, this is the first moment that Adam feels uncovered. Now spiritually nude, the man announces the absence of a covering by proclaiming his nakedness, unknowingly establishing the concept of lack in the earth. Because He represents God, Adam's words have the authority to order all created things, and with a sentence he legislates a manner of thinking that is antithetical to everything he is. Thorns begin to bud in his mind, preparing the way for those that the ground would soon produce.

Thorns are derivatives of woody plants with sharp impeding points that can serve as a hedge of protection or a defense mechanism for flowers or the fruit of a plant. Understanding these protective agents helps elucidate God's judgment on Adam. The earth was commanded to produce thorns and thistles not only to initiate Adam's toil, but also to protect itself from the one who no longer had a mindset to safeguard it. Having exchanged the mindset of kingdom wealth for an impoverished mode of thinking, Adam no longer thought like God, which is to say, He no longer spoke as Him. Creation no longer recognized this man or his voice, and as a result, the earth from which he was formed began to change, too.

As the last Adam stands in the middle of a hedge of soldiers, the sharp points of a cursed crown remind Him of that change. Ever aware that He must make humanity recognizable again, Jesus overpowers the thorns that symbolize man's corruption and the crown that represents the kingdoms He refused in the wilderness (Rev. 15:14; 19:12). When the Son of God covers the crown in blood, He transforms the image of depravity into a sign of victory.

By launching His ministry when He turned water into wine, Jesus connects the crown's prosperity to the supernatural. He begins by ordering servants to fill six pots to the brim. These pots were giant containers that held water used for purification, because cleansing was very important to Jews. In fact, a Jewish saying of that day, "He who uses much water in washing will gain much wealth in this world," teaches us that water, like wine, is associated with wealth. Through His power, Jesus converts water into wine, shifting the substance of the liquid while maintaining the sign of wealth indicated in the saying just mentioned. This transition is also visible in the crucifixion story. Jesus first sweats blood and water in Gethsemane to redeem the human will, but He sheds blood through the crown of thorns to release new wine for the mind.

Jesus prepares us for this revelation in His teaching about wineskins (Mk. 2:22). Wineskins were sacks made of sheep or goat skin that held wine. As wine underwent the fermenting process, so did the bag, causing it to harden and stiffen. If new wine was added to the hardened bag, the skin would expand beyond its limits and burst. Thus, both the wine and the container would be lost. Jesus is the lamb (sheep) whose body acts as a new wineskin that holds his blood, which signifies the new wine of a kingdom mindset. It is available to us only because the wineskin (body) was broken. This wine represents the wealth of the kingdom, which cannot be put into an old wineskin, or Adamic mindset. The thorns that pierce Jesus' head pierce the old mindset, creating apertures to pour out the wealth of the kingdom. In replacing the sweat of Gethsemane with blood from the thorny crown, the Miracle-Worker turns water to wine again.

Only with new wine and a new wineskin can we truly understand kingdom wealth. Great misunderstandings of kingdom wealth have contaminated the wine in many of our churches, so we must be vigilant about grasping God's intention for wealth by studying the ways in which it is associated with His person, presence, and power. One great illustration of that power is Israel's deliverance from Egypt.

The exodus was an earth-shaking demonstration of power that indicated deliverance from the world and its financial system. When God told Moses to instruct the Israelites to borrow gold and silver and vessels from the Egyptians, the Lord gave them so much favor that their oppressors became the funders of their exodus (Ex. 11:2, 12:35-6). By freeing the Israelites from Egyptian bondage, the Lord exhibited power over all gods, including Pharaoh, who was also considered a god. In like manner, Jesus triumphed over poverty when

He sacrificed His body and blood to restore the wealth of Eden.

Just as our wealth is connected to communion, so was Israel's connected to the Passover meal. Parallels between the Lamb of God and the Passover lamb help us see the crown's connection to communion. Like the Passover lamb selected five days before the sacrifice, Jesus entered Jerusalem five days before He was crucified. Laying down His life at 3:00 PM, Jesus died at the very time the Passover lamb was traditionally slain, showing us that He didn't just observe Passover; He fulfilled it (Lk. 2:41). Passover teaches us that the kingdom is never separate from communion, and that celebrating this covenant meal attaches seven blessings to our lives: angelic assignment (Ex. 23:20); divine protection (23:22); prosperity (23:25); healing (23:25); longevity (23:26); increase and inheritance (23:30); and a special year of blessing (23:31).

Like the children of Israel who partook of a miraculous meal and experienced a wealth transfer, we can also lay hold of God's promise for prosperity as we take communion. The Lord's Table furnishes a lavish meal of fellowship that exposes the scraps of oppressors, and the more we gather at this Table, the more we are freed of systemic and generational bondage. If every believer broke free of financial bondage, we would completely alter the global economy! This is exactly what happened in Egypt after the Israelites left and Pharaoh realized that God's people not only had the wealth, but also the knowledge to generate and maintain it (Deut. 8:18).

No longer under Egyptian control, the Israelites could see that dependence on oppressive systems strips creative thought patterns, and demands a person's influence, or voice in exchange for provisions. These systems only value voices inasmuch as they echo what those in power are already proclaiming, which explains why the Bible tells us, "the poor man's wisdom is despised, and his words are not heard (Ecc. 9:16)." Like it or not, wealth is one of the most formidable voices of our age, just as it was in the days of the exodus, because it increases ability, capacity, and scope. This is why we must learn to dissociate it from darkness, for such an assumption is a trick of the enemy used to hinder kingdom advancement. Rather, we choose to operate in God's original intent for us, which includes the wealth needed to carry His voice to four corners of the earth. As we proclaim His name, we realize that walking in the blessings of God is not only our privilege; it is our responsibility.

And Jabez called on the God of Israel saying, "Oh, that You would bless me indeed, and enlarge my territory, that Your hand would be with me, and that You would keep me from evil, that I may not cause pain!" So God granted him what he requested (1 Chron. 4:10).

Jabez caught a revelation of the blessing. To join that man on his walk in blessings, we must first step into scripture. The Hebrew term for blessing (berakah or berek) comes from the consonant root BRK, which means to overflow, or to take note of something that is larger than itself. We see this principle of blessing when God grants Jabez's request for enlarged territory. Berakah signals a greeting or benediction, and is associated with liberality, gifts, and prosperity, while berek comes from a word that means knee, which implies a falling to the knees to display honor, acknowledgement, or reverence. The concept of blessing varies a bit in the New Testament, where the Greek term for blessing, eulogia, is introduced. A word now associated with funerals, eulogia means fine speaking, commendation, consecration, and bounty. Like berek, eulogia emphasizes the proper response to one worthy of honor, and like berakah, it is in itself a generous gift expressed through the creative power of speaking.

Before we advance further into the blessing, we need to deal with the painful rock that has slipped into our shoes, into our foundational teachings on blessing and prosperity. That rock makes it difficult to walk in the blessings of God and is a painful distraction from the path already outlined for us. Somewhere along the journey we picked up the notion that wealth, riches, abundance, prosperity, money, affluence, possessions, and resources were dangerous indicators of selfishness, greed, scriptural abuse, evil, insincerity, and pride. As the gulf between seemingly prosperous leaders and impoverished followers appeared to widen, disdain for teaching on and conversation about financial success infiltrated the Body of Christ, anchored by false assumptions of Jesus' poverty and beliefs that true discipleship required such. To make matters worse, preaching about economic empowerment came under serious attack, being branded Prosperity Gospel by some Christian leaders who condemned a link between faith and prosperity. Talk about an uphill journey. We might need to sit for a moment and reflect on ways that our predecessors handled this dangerous nuisance.

Acts 8 records Peter's rebuke of Simon, a former sorcerer who attempts to buy the gift of the Holy Spirit, and Philippians 1 recounts Paul's discernment of those preaching only for personal gain. The apostles teach us that there are some who seek to misuse the Gospel for selfish ambition, prostituting the faith to gain wealth unjustly. But the two leaders also preach and live this truth – the Gospel proclaims the blood of Jesus Christ, which has redeemed every part of our lives and availed every resource needed to prosper them (Rom. 8:32). While we in no way condone the misappropriation of the Gospel, we do not deny or apologize for its inclusion of wealth. We cannot allow the impure motives of some to govern the way that we apply and proclaim the Gospel that reveals God's nature. We cannot separate Gpd from the blessing (prosperity, honor, overflow), because He is the Blesser who makes us a blessing. As we come into a greater knowledge of Him, the Lord equips us to be solutions and resource centers that manifest His purpose and demonstrate His heart. Second Peter 1:3 tells us that God has "given unto us all things that pertain unto life and godliness, through the knowledge of him that has called us to glory and virtue." The knowledge of God (Greek epignosis) allows us to operate in kingdom blessings in both natural and supernatural realms, and knowing God always go back to communion. Fellowship with the Father brings revelation of His will and nature, which we must have to maintain the blessings that the blood of Jesus has restored (Matt. 16:17).

Our journey through Scripture also uncovers three ways that blessings can be transferred: inheritance, invocation, and impartation. Inheritance transfers blessings based on lineage and bloodline (Gal. 3:16); invocation does so through the spoken word or touch (Gen. 26:1-12; Gen. 28:1-4); and impartation transfers blessings based on relationship (Matt. 13:11). Every blessing of God is not financial, but every blessing does function out of kingdom principles, and kingdom principles govern kingdom wealth. For example, the Lord has given us power to get wealth, but He also gave us a command to tithe. In God's economy, tithing is the principle foundation for blessed living. Tithers commit to take care of God's house (the local church) by giving at least ten percent of their income, and God commits to blessing them in a multitude of ways. He pulls back the curtains of heaven and flings open its windows to pour out a blessing that surpasses capacity. He stuffs Ephesians 3:20 into Malachi 3:10, wraps it in a scarlet bow and hand-delivers it to tithers, rebuking the devourer for their sake along the way. In so doing, He discloses a plan to perpetually bless them, while protecting and sustaining the blessings that He has already given.

The Lord purposed in His heart to bless humanity before He ever formed us. His first widespread demonstration of this blessing was toward the Jews, but He did not confine the blessing to them alone. Gentiles have also been grafted into the seed of Abraham through Jesus Christ, and they now have a part in receiving and being the blessing (Gal. 3:9, 14; Rom. 11:17-24). Because of Jesus' blood, Christians of every nation can lay hold of the promise that God gave to Abraham in Genesis 22:17, "In blessing I will bless thee, and in multiplying I will multiply thy seed."

When God pronounces a blessing, He does so from eternity, a realm in which there is no end. This kind of setting causes His declarations to be immediately performed and simultaneously continuous. We see this dynamic in the lives of Adam and Eve, the first humans to receive a blessing from God. God's blessing for Adam and Eve was enacted in eternity, and because His blessings cannot be revoked, He guaranteed that the first couple was always blessed (this same principle applied to Isaac, who could not rescind the blessing he bestowed on Jacob though it was intended for Esau). Unable to curse what/who He had already blessed, the Lord cursed the ground and the serpent. Having linked reproduction to Adam and Eve's blessing, God still allowed them to fill the earth although they could not fulfill the mandate tied to the blessing: "And God blessed them, and God said unto them, Be fruitful and multiply, and replenish the earth, and subdue it: and have dominion over [...] every living thing that moves upon the earth (Gen. 1:28)." Cursing Adam and Eve would have infringed on the principle of eternal blessing, and would have contradicted God's character. Because the two were made in His image, made as God, cursing them would have been like cursing Himself. However, despite the upheld blessing, Adam and Eve's sin abased them to a life beneath the realm of blessing that they originally inhabited. This abasement exposed them (and all humanity) to the effects of curses on the ground and the serpent (hard labor and a bruised heel), until the shed blood of Jesus reversed the curse and reinstated the blessing.

Come up here.

Jesus is beckoning us to ascend to new levels in the Spirit and challenging us to walk in the blessings of God. The blessings of the Lord impact us holistically, but they first affect us spiritually, for Ephesians 1:3 reminds us that God has, "blessed us with all spiritual blessings in heavenly places in Christ." We just noted that blessings originate in eternity, so we understand that we are initially blessed in the realm of the spirit, then in the natural. This realm shapes our spiritual lives and is the place in which we commune with the Father in faith.

Faith is the currency of heaven and those who are rich in it position themselves to receive wealth transfers in the earth. Having had their faith tested and tried, these believers learn to carefully manage such precious currency, all the while acquiring the ability to steward the tangible wealth of the kingdom. This explains why God's kingdom assignments always require a measure of faith, no matter what resources are available. Without the training of faith, the blessing of wealth could prove to be an unbearable burden, but with it, the blessing becomes a powerful tool used to advance the kingdom.

Through the lens of faith we better understand Proverbs 10:22, which promises that the blessing of God "makes rich, and he adds no sorrow with it." Unlike many people who are financially prosperous but spiritually destitute, those who are abundant in faith can experience God's overflow in every area of their lives as they continue to walk in the Spirit.

The spirit realm is also marked by exponential multiplication and miracles. This kind of abundance is apparent when Jesus blesses the fish and loaves and they supernaturally multiply to feed thousands (Mk. 6:41-43); when Elijah's prophecy initiates supernatural replenishment of a widow's oil until the drought ends (1 Kgs. 17:8-15); and when Elisha's command causes miraculous multiplication of oil for an obedient widow who sells it to keep her sons (2 Kgs. 4:1-7). The overflow of blessings in the spirit causes an automatic spillover in the natural. As those whom God has blessed, we have been strategically placed in neighborhoods, workplaces, schools, and various other gardens to manifest the kingdom and release the blessings of God (Gen. 39:5). As blessings overtake the environments with which we are associated, people with whom we interact will observe God's nature and be drawn to Him.

Walking in the blessings of God may feel like a long and lonely journey, but we must choose the blessing anyway, which is to say, we must choose life. Deuteronomy 30:19 tells says it this way, "I have set before you life and death, blessing and cursing: therefore choose life, that both you and your seed may live." When we choose life, we cover ourselves and the generations to come in the blessings of God, which are maintained through faith in Him and obedience to the path that His blood has outlined for us (Deut. 11:26-28). Now that we have treaded the bloody path from the whipping post to the hall, we realize that Jesus makes our way prosperous even in agony. We need the Waymaker to order our steps, especially now that our feet are heading towards Calvary.

*To clasp the hands in prayer
is the beginning of an uprising
against the disorder of the world.*

- Karl Barth, 20th Century Theologian

CHAPTER 6

Nail-Pierced Hands:
Restoration of Authority

The street is winding and narrow and full of blood. Throngs of people flock to the Via Dolorosa, the Way of Suffering, to watch Jesus carry the beam that will soon be nailed to His hands. He clings to the beam like He does to God's will; exercising the muscles He strengthened in Gethsemane. His body leaks blood all the way to Golgotha, taking a rest only to prepare for more pain. Finally, He reaches the hill and so do we. A soldier grips the flesh remaining on Jesus' hands, inadvertently triggering a flood of images in our minds… Those are the hands that overthrew the moneychangers' tables in the temple; that gripped Peter's body to rescue his life and his faith; that wrote in the dust; that formed a mud pie to heal a blind man; that restored the ear of the high priest's servant; that scrubbed filth from our feet last night; that broke bread and poured wine to commune with us. Those are the hands of a man bracing for nails.

The soldier feels for a depression between the bones near Jesus' wrists. He finds it. Selecting one of the five to seven inch nails in his quiver, he hammers wrought iron into both of the Savior's hands. Blood gushes out as if in a race to the skin's surface, coating the mangled body afresh. The fountains of blood bursting from His hands accompany the flood of tears scurrying down our faces. We cannot fathom why Jesus is suffering the type of death allotted to the worst of criminals and to slaves. How can a King be valued at the price of a slave, a mere thirty shekels of silver (Ex. 21:32), and how can he die like one in the eyes of the law?

Slaves occupied the lowest social state and were bound not only to their masters, but also to other ruling powers. Having no power in and of themselves, slaves were always under authority, but never in it. Yet, in contrast to other condemned men who suffered the death sentence of the powerless, Jesus never lost authority. He simply resisted the temptation to demonstrate it. He refused to beckon legions of angels to His aid; refused to *force* others to minister to Him. Instead, He gave His life in obedience to the Father who would soon place all authority in His hands.

Scripture teaches us that hands are indicative of authority (Greek *exousia*). They represent the power to act, and are utilized in many authoritative endeavors. They are used to ordain (1 Tim. 4:14); to confer blessings on future generations (Gen. 48:14); to overcome enemies in battle (2 Sam. 22:35); to preserve life (Est. 5:2); to conquer sickness (Lk. 4:40); and as points of contact through which people receive the Holy Ghost (Acts 8:17). The Greek term for hands, *cheiras*, also associates them with instruments used to accomplish an objective like that of sacrifice (Ex. 29:15); service (2 Kgs. 3:11); worship (1 Kgs. 8:22); or healing (Job 5:18). Hands represent both the works of God and the means by which He completes a specific purpose. Authority is the power behind the methods used, and the blood of Jesus is the power behind the purpose itself. When Jesus shed blood in His hands, He restored the authority that Adam squandered in Eden. If we journey back to that garden we will discover the authority that has been transferred to us.

Before and during creation, God's presence was the governing authority. When God made Adam in His image and authorized him to oversee all of creation, His manner of government did not change. Rather, it was transferred to Adam in the spirit of communion so that creation would respond to him just as it did to God. In this manner, to see Adam was to see the Father. Demonstrating the spiritual law that only those under authority can be in it, Adam (and Eve) maintained authority to perform and manage the works of God as long as they communed with Him. When the serpent questioned authority by tempting Eve (not just with fruit, but also with knowledge), she responded by stating God's instruction not to eat the fruit and then added the stipulation of not touching it (Gen. 2:17; 3:3). By adding to God's word, Eve used the reservoir of her intellect to attempt to strengthen God's directive, and this addition is precisely where the enemy hooked her. Adding the carnal to the spiritual taints authority and gives the devil a foothold in the mind. After the serpent realized that Eve had moved part of her thought-life out from under God's authority, he enticed the portion of her mindset that yearned for the supernatural but sought it through the flesh. This is why Eve could be hooked with a physical object, though her temptation was spiritual in nature. As she and Adam ate the fruit, they chose anarchy over authority and laid a foundation of cowardice for coming leaders like King Ahab.

When Adam ceded his authority through silence and compliance, he yielded all legal rights to his domain. Satan was able to access Adam's authority, and thereby gain control in the realm that man abides, the earth (2 Cor. 4:4; Eph. 2:2; Jn. 12:31). Consequently, God cursed the serpent for deceiving Adam and caused him to crawl on his belly, an act that stripped him of extremities. Because the arms, which held his hands (authority), and legs, which held his feet (dominion), were taken, the serpent would never be recognized as a *legitimate* ruler. So while the serpent can inflict harm, it cannot govern. This is why serpents never represent the rulers of the four domains like the lion, eagle, ox, and man do. In fact, serpents are trampled under foot (Ps. 91); consumed (Ex. 7:13); and simply shaken off (Acts 28:5). However, we must understand that though the serpent would not rule, it would be permitted to consume.

God said that the serpent would eat dust, the very substance from which man was made. Every serpent has a forked tongued that enables it to find prey through its sense of smell, the sense that is indicative of discernment. The serpent utilizes a sort of dual discernment that allows it to operate keenly for the sake of consumption. This is how the enemy so quickly finds weaknesses in the lives of God's people. Yet, if we stay under the blood, the Lord will hide us and our weaknesses so that the enemy will not be able to find them. As we dwell in the secret place of God, we take back authority through the blood of Jesus, which gives us the power and responsibility to be God's hands (extensions) in the earth as we perform His works.

The blood of Jesus is the foundation of purpose-centered work and the ultimate expression of God's purpose for humanity. Only the blood gives life and energizes purpose to bring fulfillment; works stemming from the purpose themselves cannot do so.

Engaging the works of purpose without a revelation of the blood is not only dangerous; it is rebellion. Authority should be understood in conjunction with two major tenets – the principle of God's authority and the principle of Satanic rebellion, both of which are recounted in the fall of Lucifer. Lucifer, whose name comes from the Hebrew *halal*, which means praise, to boast of oneself, or to glory foolishly, reminds us that names denote purpose and authority. When the fallen angel determines that he will ascend into heaven; exalt his throne above the stars of God; sit on the mount of the congregation; ascend above the heights of the clouds; and *be like the Most High* (Isa. 14:12-15), he stops fulfilling the purpose of praising God and begins to boast of himself. Knowing that he cannot procure authority on his own, the fallen one tries to reinvent himself (be like God) through a spirit of rebellion. Lucifer wants to take God's glory, and he hopes to get it by perverting Adam's purpose and stealing his authority.

When Satan realizes that God has created man in His image, he immediately knows that, because humans are supernatural beings, they will long to operate in the realm of the spirit. He convinces Eve that she can engage a higher dimension of the spirit through rebellion, and he offers the same notion to believers today who want to operate in gifts and anointings without a revelation of the blood. Void of this revelation, they grow hungry for glory. They feast on the praises of men, but are starved of spiritual fulfillment. This is why Satan's temptation to rebel is so appealing to them, since it offers access to the supernatural without submission to authority. Gaining a true revelation of the blood allows us to both see and participate in God's works, which are produced in the supernatural and manifested in the natural by the Holy Spirit and under the leadership to whom God has called us. These works reveal the absolute necessity to abide in the deep places of God, for there we acquire greater insight of our authority in the realm of the spirit; the state in which everything happens by the force of faith.

Faith always recognizes and observes authority (Matt. 8:5-10). We see this principle most clearly in Jesus, who was born of a woman but conceived of the Holy Ghost. As the ultimate juncture of humanity and divinity, He observed natural and spiritual laws to operate in and remain under authority. This explains why Satan tried so hard to pressure Jesus to rebel, or to act independently of God's will. In so doing, He would have relinquished authority, giving the enemy an even stronger hold in the natural and new access in the spirit. But Jesus resisted rebellion and chose to completely align himself (spirit, soul, body) with God's will. His decision to remain under authority while shedding blood cancelled every claim that Satan had to humanity, even as it stripped principalities and powers, which are the arms and legs (extremities) of the enemy (Col. 2:13-15). When Jesus harrowed hell and took the keys (access, principles) to death and Hades, He announced the complete recovery of every domain, and was recognized as One to whom all authority had been given (Matt. 28:18). In turn, Jesus gave authority to God's people through His blood and His name (Lk. 10:17-19; Eph. 1:19-23). With Him we are crucified (Rom. 6:6-7), buried and raised (Eph. 2:4-6), exalted, enthroned, and hidden (Col. 3:1-3). We are now so identified with Jesus that He calls us His body. But many ask, if we have been given the authority to operate as He did, why do we see so few demonstrations of His power?

Location, Location, Location

Adam, where are you? The cosmos is forced to absorb a new phenomenon – a question from the Holy Commander. When Adam breaks communion with God by fellowshipping with the unsanctified portion of Eve's mind, the man representing God in the earth affects the entire universe. Nothing in the created order knows how to respond to an inquiring God or a hiding ambassador. Everything stands still and waits for the man to declare his location, to articulate the spiritual, mental, and physical state of severed fellowship. Immediately the universe feels the eruption of a counter-world, the writhing pain produced by newborn sin. Leaving the womb of a rebel, the illegitimate infant knows exactly where Adam is, for it lies in the man's arms. Heaven and earth stand at attention, each recognizing that the world has just changed.

Understanding the location and instrumentality of God and His miracles is vital for walking in the Spirit. Location is always associated with the will. Jesus reveals this in His prayer to God in John 17:11 by saying, "Holy Father, keep through your own name those whom you have given me, that they may be one, as we are." The Greek translation of this petition is in the present subjunctive tense, which emphasizes the will of a person. This means that although Jesus was physically located in a sinful world, He was spiritually and mentally situated in the supernatural through His will. In like manner, we align our will with God to operate in the miraculous and produce works that bring revelation. The degree to which we are able to perform the works of Jesus (and greater ones) hinges on how closely, consistently, and dependently we abide in the world of the Father. As we become situated in the realm of the spirit, the miraculous is funneled into our lives through exhibitions of power that honor Christ's labor (Eph. 3:7; Col. 1:29).

Jesus tells us in John 14:10 that God dwells in us and is the facilitator of miraculous works. He uses these works to make Himself known in tangible, accessible ways, and to manifest the supernatural in the earth through believers who have positioned themselves to walk in the realm of the spirit. This positioning is the way that we appropriate Eden, the dwelling place of complete oneness and communion with God. That kind of habitation is what Jesus speaks to when He says, "At that day you will know that I am in my Father, and you are in me, and I am in you (Jn. 14:20)." We abide in the Father because the blood has restored our God-likeness and repositioned us in Him. As a result, we operate in the supernatural and reveal God's nature through miraculous works.

Deliverance from a carnal mind/heart is the first key to operating in the miraculous. The carnal mind hinders the supernatural by placing physical senses, intellect, and doubt above faith, so it must be replaced with a new heart that functions in faith and implements God's rhema word. The new heart is grounded in love, which is the very essence of God, and it views miracles and other demonstrations of power as acts rooted in and revealing of that love (1 Cor. 13:2). It abounds in faith to believe things not yet seen and affects multiple dimensions of existence (Heb. 11:7). In fact that faith brings a new dimension into reality, and causes the one or two dimensional context (superficial or partially visible setting) to become three-dimensional. Simply put, it pulls the word of God into a physical context through a new, believing heart, and brings the miraculous from one dimension to another. Suddenly what has been confined to the spirit and concealed in the natural becomes visible, and we are able to see God's word without obstruction (Hab. 2:1).

When Abraham obeyed in faith and went to the place that God would show him, no obstructions in the physical realm blocked him from obeying the call, because faith preserves the promise and the word prepares the way (Heb. 11:8). The rhema word went before Abraham and demolished every barrier that would seek to frustrate God's plans for the father of many nations, and faith kept the hands of the enemy from repairing these barricades. This operation calls to mind a prophetic word given to Israel:

"I will go before you, and make the crooked places straight: I will break in pieces the gates of brass, and cut in sunder the bars of iron [...] that you may know that I, the LORD, which call you by your name, am the God of Israel (Isa. 45:2-3)."

We also see the co-operation of faith and word in the life of Moses. The leader returned to Egypt by faith, and was able to govern in authority by discerning in the Spirit what was not evident in the natural. Using the rhema word of God as his substance, Moses facilitated demonstrations of power that forced the physical realm to reflect the supernatural. The natural realm aligns with the supernatural after a person's faith has done so, because nature is subject to man's authority. Faith opens a channel or portal for believing God's word alone (Mk 5:36), and when trust in God's word is the only thing flowing through this channel, maturation and consummation of that word comes into being. Thus, faith causes new creation to manifest today just as it did in the creation of heaven and earth. Nonetheless, it is *our* responsibility to oversee and carry out the work of God, which is to believe on Him whom God has sent (Jn. 6:29).

Lord, I believe. Help my unbelief.

For the most part, the struggle with faith is not an issue of will (for we want to believe), but rather an issue of method. *How* do we believe God? We will soon arrive at some principles of faith that are essential for walking in authority in the realm of the spirit, but we must first discover the foundation of faith. Romans 10:17 tells us that faith comes (exists) by hearing, and hearing comes by the (rhema) word of God. Faith is made present through hearing, the process of discerning and perceiving God's voice. One of the consequences and sin is an inability to discern that voice, which results in spiritual deafness. Those who are deaf cannot perceive the sound of their own voices, and that inability hinders speech. This same principle applies in the spirit. The enemy uses spiritual deafness to shut the mouth of the believer, so that he cannot connect with the faith that would heal him. But if the word of God reaches the inner man, it will unstop the ear and restore the ability to clearly hear the voice of the Holy Spirit and declare His it in the earth. When the believer makes a profession of faith, not only at salvation, but also with decrees that reinforce what God has already established, he steps into the authority that manifests the God-kind-of faith.

The faith of God is a three-dimensional charismatic gift encompassing the rhema word, mustard seed faith, and the power of God to manifest miracles for the sake of His kingdom. The government of God is the order of His kingdom, which Jesus compares to the mustard seed. He says that the kingdom of heaven "is like a grain of mustard seed, which a man took, and cast into his garden; and it grew, and waxed a great tree; and the fowls of the air lodged in the branches of it (Lk. 13:19; Matt. 13)." Like the kingdom, the mustard seed is ever-growing and producing, so much so that it helps meet the needs of others (e.g. lodging). The mustard seed's dimensions, substance, and essence represent God's rhema word to us. The dimension is the seed's location, the substance is the word itself, and the essence is the manifestation of faith. The substance (reality) of this rhema word becomes our reality as we believe. This means that everything contradicting God's word is unreality, which is one of the Hebrew definitions of the formless world described in Genesis 1:2. Mustard-seed faith is by nature miraculous, and when sowed into the ground of a believing heart, it produces kingdom miracles.

We seek to operate in the miraculous to advance the reign of God, and we understand that the word, the ear, and our faith must all be active to accomplish that objective. As faith directs us to the rhema word, it carves out a time of communion during which God meets us and immediately responds to our needs. He desires to constantly commune with us, but doubt interrupts that fellowship because unbelief cannot penetrate the realm of God. This is why Adam and Eve were ejected from Eden after they doubted God's word and believed that of the serpent, for the garden was a duplication of God's world. It is impossible to please God without faith because faith ethos of His environment.

Hebrews 11 teaches us that faith is the substance of things hoped for, and the evidence of things not seen. The term substance comes from two Greek words that mean to "stand under something." To function in faith is to stand under the authority of the blood of Jesus and to align ourselves with God's will in order to change the content of a thing. Authoritative and audacious, faith commands belief to infiltrate seemingly impossible circumstances and forces them to change their nature (substance) to reflect the rhema word. We see this depicted through the story of the fig tree in Matthew 11. Jesus approaches the fig tree for food, but goes hungry because it has no fruit. It is not the season to produce figs, but Jesus knows that all nature is designed to serve God's purpose, so the tree should have immediately produced to fulfill the need. It should have altered its natural response to accommodate God the Son, like the waves did when He walked on water, or like the sun did at Joshua's command (Matt. 14:25; Josh. 10:12-13). Jesus restricted the tree from ever producing again because it did not submit to (stand under) the order of the supernatural to help fill a need. In short, it resisted the miraculous. As those standing in the faith of God and under the authority of Jesus' blood, we can also superimpose the will of God and change specific regions of the physical realm through the force of faith.

Faith is God's manner of thinking; thinking is God's manner of speech, and speaking is God's manner of activity. In other words, for God, to think it is to speak it and to speak it is to be it. This explains why the faith of God is timeless, yet immediate. Every act and manifestation of faith is already complete, because God accomplished everything He intended to do for humanity before He sanctified the seventh day (Heb. 4:9-10). Our faith simply accesses what He has already done. Faith allows us to function in authority, gives us the ability to oversee and perform works, and to give commands and instructions. We see the link between faith and authority in Matthew 8 with the story of the centurion who says to Jesus, "For I am a man under authority, having soldiers under me: and I say to this man, Go, and he goes; and to another, Come, and he comes; and to my servant, Do this, and he does it." The latter part of the centurion's response is in the Greek aorist tense, which is characterized by timelessness or immediate consequence. The absence of delay between a command and an act the centurion's understanding of faith, which mirrors the faith of God. In the same way, the moment that we petition God in faith according to His rhema word, whatever we ask is instantly given (Matt. 21:22). We authorize the works of God by applying targeted faith, which is concentrated trust for God's will to be manifested in a specific area. When the centurion targets his faith toward the servant in accordance with God's will to bring healing, the servant is immediately healed. The centurion's faith determines the level at which he received from the Lord, and ours does, too.

As instruments of righteousness, we are living demonstrations of faith, power, and the supernatural. Through the blood of Jesus and the faith of God, we are positioned in the Spirit to govern the earth as His extensions (hands). As faith grows and matures in us, our own hands begin to change. Hands that used to cover eyes are now lifted in worship. Hands that were once feeble are now trained for war. They uphold the arms of leaders and rebuild broken walls; they heal the sick and pull the miraculous into the natural. These hands, your hands, are extensions of Almighty God. It's time to put them to work.

He who is destined for power does not have to fight for it.

- Ugandan proverb

CHAPTER 7

Nail-Pierced Feet:
Restoration of Dominion

*B*reathe. We just realized that eight seconds have passed since we last inhaled. Everything we have believed for is choked by the sight of His body nailed to that beam. Bright red streaks from freshly inflicted hand wounds coat the darker hues of blood that stained His body at the whipping post. Blood runs into Jesus' eyes, oozes from hollows in His flesh, and races down the side of His body to ensure that every inch of His frame has been baptized afresh. The murmurs of those who never knew Him thicken the air with temptation to abandon our Master, especially since we know what is coming next. It is time to nail His feet. Pray. The soldier begins to arrange His feet, dyeing fingertips with holy blood as he finds a place to thrust the nail. He raises his right arm and plunges it down with power, driving the spike through Jesus' soles. Blood erupts from His feet like lava from a volcano and washes away our hope for some miraculous deliverance. Weep. That is all we can do after the wooden altar is erected and Jesus' disfigured body is put on parade. The display is so horrendous that its only identifiable marker is a sign announcing Jesus' crime, "Jesus of Nazareth, King of the Jews." It takes a moment, but we finally understand the charges laid against Him. Our Messiah is guilty of having dominion.

Dominion is the state of reigning that scripture often associates with the feet. We see this connection in the Hebrew word for dominion, radah, which means, to rule, to subdue, and to tread down (another action of the feet). Feet can indicate a place of power (e.g. falling at a person's feet; Est. 8:3; 1 Sam. 25:4); can represent authority over elements (e.g. Jesus walking on water; Matt. 14:22-33); and can suggest supremacy over territory (e.g. dominating every place that the feet tread; Deut. 11:24; Josh. 1:3). As the physical foundation of the body, feet help maintain support, motion, and balance, three entities that are necessary for effective rulership. To neglect the feet is to jeopardize the body, and ultimately forfeit dominion. No single incident exhibits this progression more than the fall of man.

When the Lord made Adam and Eve, He gave them a fivefold dominion mandate that reflects life in the kingdom. They were instructed to "be fruitful and multiply; fill the earth and subdue it; and have dominion [...] over every living thing that moves on the earth (Gen. 1:28)." Their mandate was founded on spiritual laws set in place to reinforce humanity's dominion. Adam originally operated within the boundaries of these laws, but when he and Eve sinned, they broke agreement with the edicts that undergirded their status as creatures made like God. Because their image was marred, Adam and Eve lost dominion and the repercussions of evil began to manifest. A curse entered the world for the first time; sweat was created and assigned to the earth; the ground was commanded to cough up thorns and thistles instead of fruit; pain was attached to childbirth; unrestricted fellowship with God evaporated like water in the summer heat; and a covenant marriage became the only place that Adam could rule. When Adam sinned, he fractured communion with God and violated the framework (laws) that supported his dominion. So traumatic was the fall of man that no human could reverse its consequences. It would take a Great Physician who also sustained a foot injury to correct such a fall.

The blood that Jesus shed in his feet restored humanity's dominion. Through it we fulfill the fivefold mandate that manifests in specific ways. To be fruitful is to produce by converting the lost, discipling the saved, and making sons/daughters out of slaves and servants. To multiply is to increase and enlarge to further God's kingdom purpose throughout all generations. This is done by continuing to make disciples and by allowing our sons and daughters to beget others. To fill the earth is to occupy at full capacity, and to train sons and daughters in four areas: identity, destiny (purpose and calling), covenantal understanding, and revelation and impartation of their kingdom assignments. To subdue is to possess and bring under subjection by releasing sons and daughters into their respective spheres of influence. This allows individual anointings to manifest in culture to dispossess darkness and institute light. Finally, to have dominion is to govern and steward creation, ruling over specific territories so the glory of God inundates the earth to both awaken and transform the world.

Along with dominion, the blood of Jesus also restored our ability to have covenantal relationships with God and with people. Since communion with God is the foundation of the blood, we fellowship with Him while we rule. As we fulfill the fivefold mandate, we also make sure that future generations understand that the blood is the basis of God's covenant (Heb. 9:7). The blood has already provided everything we need to recover dominion and set back in order the framework of His original intent by destroying the works of the devil. The blood of Jesus freed the world from the grip of Satan (Matt. 28:18; Rev. 1:18), but the enemy still has power (might, influence) over the earth through deception and rebellion. Satan does not have power over us, but he does seek to rob us of our power through ignorance (the lack of knowledge), lethargy (the sluggish pursuit of spiritual things), and apathy (the lack of concern for and interest in spiritual things – 2 Cor. 4:4).

Ignorance is not bliss. It leads to bondage and bondage nullifies dominion, but knowledge of the Word and the Spirit helps us rule multiple domains (Hos. 4:6; Jn. 14:12-17; Matt. 11:12). Liberty is where the Spirit of the Lord is, so it is impossible to walk in the Spirit in an area and be in bondage in the same place. To walk in the Spirit is to operate in dominion, meaning that we live by faith and in triumph. No longer under Satan's influence, we have victory through the blood of Jesus and the enemy is now subject to us. By knowing and applying the truth of God, we are able to take back everything that was stolen from us. But we must know that taking back takes energy.

We are most vulnerable to lethargy and apathy when we are physically tired, emotionally drained, and spiritually naïve. With all subtlety and craftiness, these two spirits come to oppress God's people. Lethargy affected the life and reign of David, who acquired a pattern of iniquity from his ancestor Rahab. Though he was fully aware of Rahab's lifestyle, David failed to guard himself against that kind of iniquity and eventually succumbed to it with Bathsheba. As a result, iniquity was transferred to his descendants to such a degree that David's own son slept with his wives (2 Sam. 16-19). His experience reminds us that iniquitous patterns are frequently linked to covenant breaking (covenant is a marker of dominion), and often manifested through sins like adultery, anger, suicide, and abandonment. But equally dangerous is apathy. Matthew 12:43-45 teaches that the person who fails to safeguard his heart in apathy opens a door for demonic oppression, saying,

> *"When the unclean spirit is gone out of a man, he walks through dry places, seeking rest, and finds none. Then he says, I will return into my house from whence I came out; and when he is come, he finds it empty, swept, and garnished. Then goes he, and takes with himself seven other spirits more wicked than himself, and they enter in and dwell there."*

Notice that the evil spirit still views the person as his possession, saying, "I will return into my house." When the spirit comes back and finds no presence of the gospel or prayer, he brings stronger spirits to reestablish and fortify that person's heart as demonic territory. Essentially, the person escalates his own oppression by maintaining an apathetic posture. Without the blood of Jesus, the person would have no hope for deliverance.

Deliverance is closely related to dominion. When we consider a Greek term for dominion, archo, which means to reign, rule over, to be first, chief, or leader, we see that dominion is impossible without deliverance. We cannot rule over what imprisons us, and we cannot lead that which orders us. Through prophetic insight we understand the need for dominion and deliverance over the next several years, which will revolve around time and timing. God is going to open windows of opportunity that are appointed for kingdom advancement, and we must be alert and attentive to access them. To operate in a higher level of kingdom assignment, we have to become a sharper, spirit-led body. We must walk in deliverance.

Deliverance is the most misunderstood and least practiced demonstration of power, though Jesus dedicated a third of His ministry it. Deliverance is not just freedom from bondage; it is also freedom to operate, for where it is practiced, revival is present. When deliverance comes to a specific territory, revival also comes to loose gifts and anointings that advance the kingdom of God. Hence, the ministry of deliverance works presently to destroy strongholds and progressively to spread the gospel in various ways. We should be aware that Satan has a similar strategy. He uses demons to hold people captive, in hopes that they will be used to ensnare others. He understands that spiritual principles and objectives are driven by the advancement of a kingdom, because one person actually represents a much greater people. We see this most explicitly in Jesus, who simultaneously represents all of humanity and divinity. It is also evident in the naming of Israel, which transitions one man into a entire nation of people; in Jacob's sons, most of whom become the tribes of Israel; and even in God's equation of one day to a thousand years (2 Pet. 3:8). Because one entity is indicative of a greater whole, we cannot stop at individual deliverance alone. We must bring it to the entire generation so we can all fulfill the dominion mandate. To do so, we need to know how the inner workings of bondage try to hinder that purpose.

Satan can only gain access to our lives in two ways – intrusion and legal ground. Intrusion is the act of pushing, thrusting, or forcing in without permission or invitation, and it only accounts for about five percent of our problems. Acts of intrusion are fiery darts, or external attacks that have no legal right to touch us. Satan intrudes to turn our attention from God so we can break communion with Him by focusing on (fellowshipping with) the problem at hand. To resist the enemy and his intrusion, we focus on and praise God, ensure that we have given the devil no place, and pray for Gods' wisdom, power, presence, and plan as we put on our spiritual armor (Jas. 4:7-8; Eph. 6:12-18).

Legal ground is much more complex, widespread, and subtle than intrusion. It is an area that Satan has a right to be present and active because he has been given access or place. Ephesians 4:27 warns us to not give place to the devil, because that access becomes the epicenter of divination and witchcraft that, when continuously engaged, gives legal ground. Satan can acquire ground directly from someone who has given him place (not resisted him) or from an individual granting access on another person's behalf (e.g. mother who exposes children to demonic activity). However, it is most often availed without knowledge. Because most legal ground is ceded out of ignorance, many people don't even recognize that Satan has territory in their lives. They simply believe that the enemy's territorial rule is a part of their existence.

Legal ground can be difficult to recover because it can easily underlie seemingly innocent aims. For example, Jacob sought a blessing from his father, but he obtained it through deception. His tendency to deceive stemmed from the legal ground that his forefather, Abraham, gave up when he deceived Pharaoh and Abimelech by saying that Sarah was his sister (Gen. 12:10 20; 20:1-14). Generations later, Jacob himself is deceived about his wife (Gen. 29:21-28). Since the majority of legal ground is not easily identifiable, we should be vigilant about exploring the five access points through which it can be availed to the enemy: disobedience (willful sin); inner vows and judgments; curses;

emotional trauma; and unforgiveness. We will briefly discuss each of these.

Disobedience

Disobedience is rebellion. When God commands Saul to completely destroy the Amalekites and their belongings, he only partially obeys, preserving the choice belongings and the king to use for his own purposes. As a result, God rejects Saul as king. The man's pride and arrogance lead to disobedience, which grows into rebellion (1 Sam. 15). When people continue in rebellion, they give increasing control to demonic powers. This is why rebellion is as witchcraft. Rebellion can be elusive, but it is often revealed in initial responses. It masks bad attitudes with half-hearted submission, like the person who agrees to serve the church, but always comes late, leaves early, and complains while there. It lurks behind judgmental or critical thoughts of spiritual leaders and it questions or rejects the instructions of authority figures. When the worship leader asks everyone to stand, rebellion remains seated with arms folded. It hides behind excuses for consistent disregard of guidelines, like the man who is late to work every day or late to church every week. Rebellion hardens the heart to the point that only the Holy Spirit can soften it or create a new one (Ps. 51:10). So we pray that the Holy Spirit would engulf those acting in rebellion and create hearts of flesh that stand in awe of God's ways and wisdom. We also pray that they would come to obey God immediately, honor Him above all else, seek His heart, and follow His will. While we do not lower our standard to accommodate disobedience, we are aware that every sin has the capacity to become a stronghold, or a power-base fortified by demonic forces in the soul or body that stems from this gradual progression: Experience > Emotions > Thoughts > More Emotions > More Thoughts > Actions

> Habits > Patterns > Lifestyle > Stronghold. We must plead the blood of Jesus to interrupt and overcome this progression, and continue in prayer and communion as we sever the spirit of rebellion off of our lives and generation.

Inner Vows

Inner vows are a series of determinations rooted in emotions that are made in response to a person, experience, or desire. Evident in phrases that begin like this- "When I have children they will never…" "If that were my husband I wouldn't…" and "I will never be like my…" these vows are made to oneself and are typically based on judgments of others (Rom. 2:1; 14:4). Inner vows impose expectations that are based on a personal response, not on God's word. Like Eve, who sought to augment God's thoughts with her own, inner vows employ the wrong means to achieve a goal, and therefore, create methods that become access points for the enemy. Inner vows resist the normal process of maturation by linking people to past experiences or future ideals in an unhealthy way.

Like inner vows, unwarranted commitments originate in the carnal mind. Unwarranted commitments are internal pledges that are usually made out of deep pain and disappointment. In an effort to avoid additional pain, people make these commitments and depend on their own strength to fulfill them. By relying on themselves, those who make unwarranted commitments unknowingly produce thoughts that exalt themselves against the knowledge of God (Matt. 5:33-37; 2 Cor. 10:4-6).

The effects of these commitments can lie dormant for some time, but they ultimately transfer from one relationship to another. Vows of this sort seem to be most powerful when they involve judgments against parents, and those judgments often bleed into marital relationships. In like manner, vows against biological siblings can inhibit relationships with spiritual brothers and sisters. We break inner vows by first asking the Holy Spirit to reveal them, and then by asking God to deal with the root issue behind the personal vow. We apply the blood of Jesus to the heart and mind, and cast down every thought that exalts itself. Finally, we continuously renew our mind with the word and commune with God to prevent these vows from being reestablished in our thinking.

Curses

A curse is an oath that calls down evil on a person or thing. Like legal ground, curses can be passed down from previous generations or can be the result of individual decisions (Gal. 3:10-14). An example of this transfer is the curse of illegitimacy, which lasts for ten generations. We see this transfer in the life of Ruth, who breaks the curse of illegitimacy as a tenth generation descendant of Lot (Deut. 23:2). Curses also cause a bent toward certain sins and bondages in the bloodline, which we see in Samuel's lineage when Saul asks the witch of Endor to call up a familiar spirit. It seems that this tendency was already in Samuel's family line, because no witch has the power to call someone out of God's presence.

The tendency toward evil is called iniquity, and it manifests in a system of behaviors and consequences (Ex. 20:1-5; Deut. 5:9; Num. 14:18; 1 Kgs. 21:29). These behaviors and consequences can indicate that a curse is in operation, particularly if several factors are present or one tends to recur repeatedly. Let's review some of them:

- Mental and/or emotional breakdown (Deut. 28:28)

- Repeated or chronic sicknesses, especially if hereditary (Deut. 28:22-35, 59)

- Barrenness, a tendency to miscarry, or related female problems (Deut. 28:18)

- Marital breakdown and family alienation (Deut. 28:41; Mal. 4:5-6)

- Continual financial insufficiency (Deut. 28:17, 29, 47, 48)

- Being accident-prone (Deut. 28:29)

- History of suicides and unnatural or untimely deaths (Deut. 28:26, 45, 53, 56)

Curses can be transmitted by words (word curses) and various other means, one of which is physical objects (Jas. 3:9-10; Prov. 11:9). Physical objects can become vehicles for the spiritual power through which curses or blessings can be transferred, because an invisible force lies behind every object. If that force is not of God, it will ensnare a person wherever there is an opening. This is why God commands Israel on several occasions to destroy all of the inhabitants and plunder of cities overtaken. It is also why Achan, his family, and all of his belongings had to be expunged from the congregation of Israel (Josh. 7). If anything had remained, so would the spirit behind the curse. Objects attached to an evil spirit can become hindrances to deliverance and dominion, so we must ask God to reveal anything that keeps us in bondage and out of rulership. We purge our homes and possessions of anything to which we have inordinate affection or an unhealthy emotional tie, and anything linked to generational bondage or witchcraft. However, to ensure that we do not to trespass the boundary God has set for us in the spirit, we do not destroy objects that belong to our spouse. Rather, we plead the blood of Jesus over our family, because it gives us power to reverse every curse. To reverse the curse, we build an altar (sanctify and dedicate something to God), sow a seed, and pray. Then we nullify every negative declaration spoken about or against us by decreeing God's word in its stead. Finally, we remain cognizant of some acts and responses that can cause curses, such as:

- Rebellion and disobedience (Deut. 11:26-28)
- Making images for religious purposes or acknowledging and/or worshipping false gods (Ex. 20:4-5; Gen. 31:32, 35:16-19)
- Not hearing and obeying God's voice (Deut. 28:15-68)
- Being out from under authority or in rebellion to authorities (Rom. 13:1-2; Heb. 13:17)
- All involvement with the occult (1 Sam. 15:23; Gal. 5:20-21)
- Disrespect to parents (Eph. 6:1-3)
- All forms of oppression or injustice, especially when directed against the weak and the helpless (Deut. 27:17-19)
- All forms of illicit or unnatural sex (Deut. 27:20-23)
- Anti-Semitism (Gen. 12:3)
- Legalism, carnality, or apostasy (Jer. 17:5-6; Rom. 8:2)

- Theft or perjury (Zech. 5:1-4)

- Withholding from God money or other material resources to which He has claim (Mal. 3:8-9)

- Self-imposed curses (Matt. 12:36-37)

- Pledges or oaths that bind people to ungodly associations (Ex. 23:32)

- Curses sent by witches, warlocks, witch doctors, etc. (Eze. 13:17-23)

- Carnal talk directed against other people (Jas. 3:14-15)

- Manipulative prayers that accuse or seek to control others (Prov. 28:9)

Emotional Trauma

Emotional trauma is severe woundedness that causes lasting damage to the psychological, spiritual, or emotional development of a person. Often caused by a sudden physical injury or emotional shock, these hurts can affect an individual's outlook on people, settings, and particular environments. If left unhealed, the wounds can become doors for demonic oppression. Some of these wounds also stem from physical, mental or sexual abuse; violence; ambush; abandonment, accidents; rape; rejection; fearful experiences; the death of close family members; ungodly domination/control; divorce; and near-death experiences. Whether emotional trauma results from choices made by the individual or from the decisions of another, God's supernatural healing is absolutely essential for taking back territory from the enemy (Isa. 61:2-3). God's healing is like a balm that needs to be applied consistently over time. To heal emotional trauma, we seal off the soulish realm (mind, will, emotions) with the blood of Jesus and secure our gates (eyes, ears, mouths, etc.) We also ask the Holy Spirit to reveal triggers that jeopardize our sense of security, and to teach us how to guard our heart and keep it pure. In chapter nine we will speak more explicitly about how to participate in the healing of emotional wounds, but employing the commands just listed will help us begin to take back dominion without engaging sins like rebellion and unforgiveness.

Unforgiveness

Unforgiveness is the refusal to release a debt or an offense. Purposed to steal dominion through torment and bondage, it locks the offended person in a state of fear and suspicion in the name of protection, while it partners with other spirits like control, anxiety, and isolation to break healthy relationships and hinder godly covenants. Unforgiveness has no power over us without our consent, and since God has forgiven us, we have no right to withhold forgiveness from others (Col. 3:13). To forgive, we first recognize unforgiveness as a spirit, which means that we cannot abolish it through our own strength or flesh. When we call on the power of Jesus' blood, the Holy Spirit begins to transform and yield our heart as He channels forgiveness into it. As unforgiveness is purged and offense is released, the state of the offended person prior to any wrongdoing is restored (dominion), even if the damaged relationship is not. Then the renewed person blesses and prays for the offender, completely sealing off the access point of unforgiveness so he may fully walk in dominion (Matt. 5:44; Lk. 6:28; Rom. 12:1).

One of our greatest lessons in deliverance and dominion comes from an ancient woman who approaches Jesus from behind. After washing His feet with her tears, she makes a mop of her hair to dry the salty flood. Her kisses of repentance coat the Master's feet before ointment does, and then she breaks open the aroma of dominion that fragranced Eden, and Jesus recognizes the scent of Heaven in the earth. He delivers the woman from bondage to sin, and changes her state from dejection to dominion only days before the blood from His feet would accomplish the same for us. His deliverance reminds us that destiny is never apart from dominion, and that dominion is never apart from the blood.

Man's sin is in his failure to live what he is.

- Abraham Joshua Heschel, Rabbi, Jewish Theologian

CHAPTER 8

Bruises:
Redemption from Iniquity

There's nothing left to do now but wait. The last three years have taught us that discipleship demands that we follow Him – even when that means standing still. Today it means that we wait. We wait while soldiers vie for souvenirs of the Messiah's mantle. We wait as He hangs in agony and welcomes a new disciple. We wait while the bruises on His body change from a terrible red to a dreadful purple. We wait as Life dies before our very eyes.

What we do not have to wait for anymore is the manifestation of Isaiah's words. *He was wounded for our transgressions; He was bruised for our iniquities.* The prophet's oracle reminds us that the whole world has been waiting on the Messiah, longing for the salvation and deliverance of Yeshua. So, the least that we can do is wait *with* Him, bruised and bloody as He is.

Bruises are the result of internal bleeding that is triggered by an external force. They occur when blood vessels encounter trauma that causes blood to seep into surrounding tissue under the skin. Normally very sensitive to pressure, bruises reveal damage that is tied to blood beneath the surface. As we study correlations between bruises and iniquities, we will better comprehend how the blood shed beneath Jesus' skin addresses issues in our bloodline.

To understand iniquity, we must first understand sin. Many of us have heard the terms sin, transgression, and iniquity used interchangeably, but a closer study of these terms reveals that the words differ and actually represent varying levels of falling short of God's glory (Rom. 3:23). We see this difference in passages like Exodus 34:6-7, which states, "The LORD, The LORD God, merciful and gracious, longsuffering, and abundant in goodness and truth, Keeping mercy for thousands, who forgives *iniquity* and *transgression* and *sin* (Emphasis added)." The distinction among sin, transgression, and iniquity in this text calls our attention to a more thorough analysis of each word.

The word sin comes from an English term that is associated with archery. If an archer missed the target at which he was shooting, the overseeing authority would shout "Sin." Accordingly, sin is related to missing the mark. This is the reason that Romans 3 couples it with falling short. Sin is often identified as a single response, offense, or event, but it can be much more subtle. Sin is also straying from God's path. This deviation makes it impossible to meet a mark that can only be reached with proper positioning. While the Bible lists numerous references to acts of sin committed against God, it narrows the descriptive scope of sin to only a few definitions. Sin is unrighteousness (1 Jn. 5:17); anything that is not of faith (Rom. 14:23); the thought of foolishness (Prov. 24:9); and a refusal to do what is good (Jas. 4:17). Scriptural definitions of sin seem to merge action and deviation, thus linking sinful responses to waywardness. However, sin does not always suggest a deliberate divergence from God's law or a neglect of divine instruction.

The Bible tells us that sin can be an unintended breach of God's word committed out of ignorance or by accident (Lev. 4:13). For example, the book of Numbers teaches us that individuals whose actions resulted in the accidental death of a person were not punished under the law like those who had purposely committed murder, though both offenders sinned. Whether an act or a deviation, a conscious violation or an unintentional one, sin always makes us aware of areas in our lives that need to be aligned with and covered by the blood of Jesus. If the sin committed is not connected to iniquity, it can be addressed through confession and forgiveness and typically avoided from that point on. However, if sin is tied to iniquity, it will likely be recurring and difficult to avoid, and will first manifest in the form of a transgression.

Unlike sin committed inadvertently, transgressions are intentional revolts against God, or deliberate acts of rebellion and deviation. The Hebrew understanding of a transgression is a willful insurgence against God's path, not just His instruction at a particular moment, while the Greek interpretation of a transgression involves an overstepping of boundaries and limitations (trespassing). This is what Aaron and Miriam did when they grumbled against Moses and suggested that God could deal with them as He did with the great leader (Num. 12). They crossed a spiritual boundary of order against the Lord and His servant, so God imposed punishment immediately to address the transgression and to correct the brother and sister of

Moses. If the two had continued in this transgression, they would have uncovered iniquity.

Repeated transgressions are anchored in iniquity, and that repetition strengthens the transgressor's captivity to it. Consequently, the person escalates from unintended sin to dangerous acts of rebellion, which, as we mentioned before, is as witchcraft (1 Sam. 15:23). For this reason, it becomes much harder for him to stop committing the violation, even if he desires to do so. We hear this struggle articulated by the Apostle Paul, who says,

> *"For I do not do the good I want to do, but the evil I do not want to do—this I keep on doing. Now if I do what I do not want to do, it is no longer I who do it, but it is sin living in me that does it (Rom. 7:19-20, emphasis added)."*

As the transgression continues and bondage increases, so does the strength of iniquity. Iniquity is the catalyst behind the transgression, and the force that propels and undergirds it. It is the tendency to do wrong and the appetite for offense. Iniquity comes from the Hebrew word *avon*, a term that indicates something perverted, twisted, or not straight. This explains why iniquity is best defined as evil, perversion, and distortion. Scripture also associates iniquity with mischief (Ps. 28:3); unrighteousness (Eze. 18:24); rebellion (Dan. 9:5); corruption (Hos. 9:9); stubbornness (1 Sam. 15:23); hypocrisy (Isa. 32:6); and oppression (Eze. 18:18) -- all dispositions that contest order and alignment. The aim of iniquity is to bring disorder and contamination to multiple areas of an individual's life, and ultimately, to his entire generation. It works by appealing to the flesh, the carnal mindset that is revealed through actions in the body. Because iniquity is connected to perversion, iniquitous acts are usually abnormal, embarrassing, and shameful. Thus, those who commit them tend to conceal the acts, keeping them under the surface of sin like bruises under the skin.

The effects of hidden deeds are only compacted by a negative change in the person's beliefs, attitudes, and behaviors. That kind of shift suggests an alteration in the spiritual DNA, which can be transferred to future generations and linked to previous ones. This is how secret sins like idolatry, greed, jealousy, fear, and manipulation pass from one generation to the next. It is also how sexual perversions travel through a bloodline, manifesting as homosexuality, infidelity, molestation, rape, pedophilia, sodomy, incest, and prostitution.

The consequences of iniquity can impact countless generations and can be traced through specific patterns that recur in the bloodline. As we alluded to in the previous chapter, medical complications (hereditary diseases), physical impairments, premature deaths, systemic poverty, relationship problems, repeated imprisonment, and even perpetual unemployment or underemployment are all examples of the effects that iniquity can have on a bloodline. Effects like these can be the immediate consequence of iniquity in our own lives or the result of choices that our fathers made. The word declares,

"I, the LORD your God, am a jealous God, visiting the iniquity of the fathers on the children, on the third and the fourth generations of those who hate Me, but showing loving-kindness to thousands, to those who love Me and keep My commandments (Ex. 20:3-6)."

God does not hold us accountable for the sin of our ancestors, but scripture does teach us that their iniquities can affect our bloodline. To be clear, iniquity cannot affect our salvation, for the blood of Jesus provides it, and the Holy Spirit seals it. Iniquity cannot touch our spirit, which belongs to God, but it can affect our soul and body, and thus, affect our quality of life. Finally, since iniquity concerns underlying attitudes and postures, it can impact our nature, though it cannot replace it. For this reason, we must make a distinction between ourselves and iniquity, being careful not to use negative tendencies and behaviors as markers of identity. The areas that we have a particular bent toward evil are blood injuries under the surface that need to be addressed by the blood of Jesus, not personality traits with which we must live. Only the blood of Jesus can heal the spiritual bruises resulting from a leak of Adamic blood, and free our lineage of its susceptibility to future injuries.

The Blood

The blood of Jesus is a cleansing agent that should be understood in a Levitical sense. Priests of the Old Testament were responsible for offering sacrifices on behalf of Israelites, and for pronouncing cleansing upon those who were experiencing some type of issue, be it related to sickness, to the physical body, or to sin. Only after the priest pronounced a person clean could he or she reenter the community and receive the benefits of membership. In the same manner, Jesus stands as both the perfect sacrifice and the High Priest who accomplishes and announces our cleansing from sin, iniquity, and transgression, and Leviticus offers instruction about applying the blood to these three entities:

> *"And Aaron shall lay both his hands upon the head of the live goat, and confess over him all the **iniquities** of the children of Israel, and all their **transgressions** in all their **sins**, putting them upon the head of the goat, and shall send him away by the hand of a fit man into the wilderness (Lev. 16:21, emphasis added)."*

Just as the scapegoat bore the sins of Israel, so Jesus bore the sins of all humanity. He is the Lamb of God whose blood makes atonement for us, and the High Priest who declares us clean on earth before men and in heaven before the Father. When Jesus sprinkled blood in heaven He sealed an eternal covenant with humanity, based not on the blood of bulls or goats, but of Himself (Heb. 9:12). Because His blood has covered us, everything that it provides and represents now rests on our lives. Notwithstanding, we must appropriate the blood to operate in that fullness.

The blood of Jesus is often applied generally to sin, but not specifically to transgression or iniquity. Initially we see how to apply blood by researching Passover. During this feast, the blood was applied in three places – on the two side posts and on the upper doorpost of each Israelite home (Ex. 12:7). These three places marked the areas that the blood must now be applied for protection and deliverance. Since houses represent lives and doors represent access, when the blood was applied to the doorposts of the house, it restricted death's access and spared the lives of each person inside of the home. Conversely, if the blood was not applied to the doorposts of a home, death could enter. In the same way, when we neglect to apply the blood to the doorposts of our lives, we allow iniquity to enter our bloodline and access future generations.

A bloodless door is an access point for sin, which broadens the path for transgression and iniquity. This is exactly what happened in Cain's life. The Bible tells us that sin was crouching at Cain's door (Gen. 4:7). It sought to destroy the firstfruit of Adam and Eve in order to establish a pattern of broken communion *within* the household. This would hinder subsequent generations from having a clear vision of concurrent fellowship with God and man, and tear down the foundation of the community, the family. Abel posted blood on the doorpost of his life through the blood sacrifice that he offered to God, but his brother did not. Sin entered Cain's door (his mind and heart) with but one agenda – destruction, and that aim was satisfied when Abel's blood was spilled. The sinful act further poisoned an already toxic bloodline, and today that poison continues to manifest through murder, needless violence (the devaluing of life), hatred, and word curses.

We address sin through the blood of Jesus because it is the only agent that can restore and redeem us. It helps safeguard the lifestyle of communion that maximizes our operation in the spirit and liberates us from bondage in the natural. The blood has already broken the power of sin, transgression, and iniquity from our lives; but at times, it must be intentionally and intensely applied to areas that have been severely broken (especially those broken for generations). It is not a lack of power in the blood that warrants this consistent application, but rather our need to fully align ourselves with the blood. Proper alignment confirms that we are positioned to receive everything the blood has provided for us. This means that knowing how to apply the blood is critical for our power and prosperity.

Leviticus 26 gives specific instruction for confessing iniquity through the blood;

"If they shall confess their iniquity, and the iniquity of their fathers, with their trespass which they trespassed against me, and that also they have walked contrary unto me; And that I also have walked contrary unto them, and have brought them into the land of their enemies; if then their uncircumcised hearts be humbled, and they then accept of the punishment of their iniquity […] I will remember the covenant with their fathers (Lev. 26:40-41, 45)."

The instructions and promises listed above are still applicable today. We would do well to familiarize ourselves with their content. Let's discuss them now.

1. WE CONFESS OUR INIQUITY.

The first step in applying the blood of Jesus is being honest about the presence of iniquity in our lives and in our bloodline. The act of confessing iniquity not only declares our need for the blood of Jesus, but also uncovers the iniquity and perversion that seek to remain concealed in our nature. This helps us make a spiritual and psychological delineation between the new nature that God gives us and the former nature fueled by Adam's sinful blood. As we confess the iniquities of which we are aware, we also ask the Holy Spirit to reveal those that we have not yet considered. The more we confess, the deeper our communion with the Lord. We can fellowship with Him without fear because we know that if we confess our sins, He is faithful to forgive us (1 Jn. 1:9).

2. WE CONFESS THE INIQUITIES AND TRANSGRESSIONS OF OUR FATHERS.

Confessing the iniquities and transgressions of our fathers cleanses the bloodline of residue that could keep us and our descendants in bondage. Many of us do not know the fullness of our family's history because secret sins like to remain hidden, however, we can address the qualities that uncover iniquity, just as we can observe recurring patterns over generations. But even more than depending on our awareness and observations, we depend on the Holy Spirit to disclose the iniquities of our fathers. However, we must be careful not to investigate iniquity on our own accord to ensure that we are equipped to handle the opposition that iniquity can bring. The Holy Spirit only reveals as much as we have the capacity to properly steward, so we cannot expect to handle in His spirit what we have sought out in our flesh.

3. CONFESS GOD'S LEGITIMACY IN CHARGING US WITH INIQUITY.

As we confess our sin and prepare to be realigned with the blood, kingdom principles, and divine order, we also recognize that the punishment for sin is just. Without the blood of Jesus, we would have to pay a penalty of death (Rom. 6:23). Confessing God's justice and acknowledging the gravity of sin does not diminish the grace of God or the sacrifice of Jesus. On the contrary, it strengthens our appreciation of that grace. If we keep our focus on God, and not on iniquity, we will honor Him with true repentance, which is a change of heart and behavior.

4. APPLY THE BLOOD OF JESUS TO RECEIVE FORGIVENESS.

The blood frees us from bondage to sin, and God's forgiveness frees us from captivity to the offense. Every sinful offense tries to build a memorial to itself, a monument that becomes greater each time the memory of that violation comes to us. When we meditate on the memory of sin, we preserve the very monument that Jesus' blood has already torn down. Applying the blood annihilates the power of the monument in our lives, and receiving and walking in forgiveness keeps it from ever being erected again. In fact, one description of the Greek word *forgive* means "to send away." This term is

BRUISES: INIQUITY

used in Luke 22:34, when Jesus says, "Father, forgive them." Jesus was asking the Father to send away the memory of the people's offense, not only so they would be pardoned, but also so future generations would not suffer the effects of such a grave offense. In essence, He was healing bruises before they could ever form.

Examining forgiveness requires that we study the levels of falling short. The Bible often says that sin is forgiven, that transgressions are blotted out, and that iniquities are pardoned. Forgiveness is a rejection of the offense (as though it never happened), and blotting out covers a mark to make it unrecognizable, but pardoning concerns the offender more than it does the offense, because it clears the person from the punishment due him. The variation suggests that forgiving and blotting out demonstrate God's grace, but pardoning displays His mercy. This application of grace and mercy reflects the components of a person. Sin, which is forgiven, is associated with the soul, and transgression, which is blotted out, is associated with the body and its deeds, but iniquity, which is pardoned, relates primarily to the spirit. The Lord handles the spirit differently than He does the soul and body, because our spirit is His own. It belongs to Him.

5. ASK GOD TO RESTORE ALL THAT HAS BEEN LOST OR TAKEN AS A RESULT OF INIQUITY.

Applying the blood of Jesus to every place of sin and iniquity that the Holy Spirit brings to us accomplishes three things. First, it seals off the door from any demonic access. Next, it reinforces resistance against future attempts to access our lives. And lastly, it restores that area back to the original intent of God. Restoration addresses iniquity in both its original state and its heightened forms of manifestation. This is one reason that Jesus, the Restorer of our soul, was the seed of David, a man whose iniquity quickly progressed from adultery to murder, but whose repentance made room for complete restoration. In praying for a new heart and a right spirit, David asked for restoration of God's original intent (Ps. 51). From him we learn that iniquities must be replaced with righteousness to maintain the renewal that the blood avails.

A New Paradigm

Earlier we discussed how generations could be affected by the iniquitous actions of their fathers, and we will now see how Jesus introduced a new blood paradigm to address those deeds. Jesus never had his earthly father's blood, which is to say, He never had Adam's blood. However, He was still considered part of Joseph's lineage. In Judaism, the mother determines the child's Jewish status, but the father determines his tribal affiliation. Jesus was conceived of the Holy Ghost, but He was related with Joseph, a Judahite because the Messiah had to be a son of David (Jer. 33:17-22; 1 Chron. 17:11-14). As the Lion of the tribe of Judah, Jesus was confronted with issues in the bloodline that had harmed countless generations. Understanding the ways in which He dealt with and responded to those issues even before shedding His blood will help us appropriate the blood and its paradigm for life.

Jesus first encountered issues in the bloodline during His temptation in the wilderness, because our greatest temptations parallel issues in the blood. All three temptations urged Jesus to prove

His divinity by engaging His humanity. The first of these temptations involved food, just as the temptation in the Garden, and it sought to address communion. Jesus understood that any connection with food or a meal would signal communion, so He refused to fellowship with the enemy. Satan knew that Judah, the son of Israel (Jacob) and the ancestor of Jesus, was known for severing fellowship for personal gain. Judah broke fraternal communion with Joseph when he convinced the other brothers to sell the favored child into slavery; he broke household communion with his brothers when he departed from them (Gen. 38:1); and he broke divine communion with God when he chose to marry a Canaanite woman against the Lord's instruction. Judah's tendency to break fellowship manifested itself in his son, Onan, who refused to redeem Tamar. Yet, when Jesus chose to commune with God by refusing to indulge Satan's first temptation, He severed the misuse of fellowship from the bloodline.

In the second temptation Jesus was challenged to throw himself down and trust angels to catch Him. This temptation was about manipulation and control, which are two other manifestations of iniquity evident in the life of Judah. After the deaths of his two sons, Er and Onan, Judah commands Tamar to remain a widow until his final son is old enough to redeem her, but he actually has no intention for her redemption (Gen. 38). His deception is an attempt to manipulate her thinking and control her behavior. Centuries later, Judah's descendant, David, employs that same form of manipulation and control to have Uriah murdered; David's son, Amnon uses it to rape his half-sister, Tamar (2 Sam. 13:14); and Absalom uses it to have Amnon killed (2 Sam. 13:28-29). If Jesus had thrown Himself down (demonstrating a fall of the last Adam) to simply prove that the angels would protect Him, He would manipulated Himself. As the Word of

God, Jesus had no reason to test the validity of Scripture; both He and Satan knew how the angels would respond. To test the word would have been to try Himself, . for the sake of self-ambition. When Jesus resisted this temptation, He cleansed from the bloodline self-manipulation, which occurs when people take on iniquity as identity, and therefore, learn to live a lie.

In the final temptation Jesus was offered all kingdoms of the earth if He would worship Satan, and this test speaks to Judah's idolatry. After he married a Canaanite woman, Judah's lineage became known for their idolatrous practices. The prophet Jeremiah pronounces their idolatry when he speaks in the stead of God; "I gave faithless Israel her certificate of divorce and sent her away because of all her adulteries. Yet I saw that her unfaithful sister Judah had no fear; she also went out and committed adultery (Jer. 3:8-9)." Judah's inclination to break communion was the stimulus of his idolatry, and many generations of his descendants carried that same attribute. Solomon and his son, Rehoboam, are just two examples. When Jesus refused to worship Satan, He cleansed the appetite for idolatry from Judah's bloodline, and satisfied the hunger for an ever-present God with a meal made of His own body and blood.

The blood of Jesus completed the work that began long before He went to the cross. His blood dealt with issues in the bloodline without exposing the descendants who were working through them, and today it does the same for us. Like the disciples who remained with Jesus throughout the crucifixion, the blood waits with us when we are bruised. It eradicates iniquity and binds up the wounds inflicted by sin, while training us to receive the Healer who brings wholeness to our generation.

*What can make me whole again?
Nothing but the blood of Jesus.*

- Robert Lowry (1826-1899), Pastor, Songwriter

CHAPTER 9

A Pierced Side:
Healing of Emotional Wounds

It is finished. Jesus utters the most dreadful words we have ever heard and then bows His head in honor to the Father. He breathes over creation as God did into Adam and finally gives up the ghost. The sound of fresh heartbreak rushes from the earth to the heavens, as cries of desperation bombard the throne-room. Heaven responds with a violent earthquake that sanctions the finished work, while shaking us into alignment with the will of God.

We stay near the cross in agonizing loyalty, and watch the soldier approach with spear in hand. He shoves it into our Lord's side with a furious thrust. He's got to make sure our dream is dead. The deep gash emits blood and water onto the corpse, christening the body that will soon be resurrected. Only then do we realize that the blood outlives every wound, especially those that are meant to kill.

The last wound that Jesus bore was in His side, a place indicative of covering and agreement. The side is a place not typically exposed, and it represents vulnerable areas and experiences that are not readily visible. Covered by trusted companions who walk beside us in agreement, these areas are guarded from senseless wounds by the strength of spiritual awareness and singleness of heart. And yet, even the most faithful attendants cannot prevent the infliction of every emotional wound. Emotional wounds are deep lesions in the heart that can hinder both communion with God and ministry to people if left unchecked. These wounds are so severe that they can only be healed through the blood of Jesus.

In this chapter, we will see the healing power of Jesus' blood as we survey seven wounds frequently experienced in ministry. We will also learn how to apply the blood to emotional injuries, and how to model responses that lead us to wholeness. But before we delve into this discussion, I'd like to share a story with you…

I first met Him during my senior year of high school. He told me that His name was Rapha, and that He had come to bind up my wounds. "What wounds?" I asked. I had a loving family, a great community, and a secure future. I was trying to convince Him that I was well when I got word that my grandfather had had a massive heart attack. Never sick and always sharp, he fell dead two weeks shy of his 100th birthday. I covered the injury as best I could and used all of the tactics that church had taught me. Rapha remained present. In the same month, my mom was hospitalized for a blood clot and soon diagnosed with cancer of the liver. Chemotherapy and radiation stripped the hair that once cascaded down her back as cancer took a tall, robust woman to eighty pounds in five months. When my mother, my best friend, took her last breath, Rapha breathed into me. Pain was trying to suffocate my soul and only

PIERCED SIDE: EMOTIONAL WOUNDS

He could contend for my life. When the church said that my mom's sickness and death were God's will, He ached at words so untrue. He knew I believed them. He remained quiet as I hurled accusations at Him; continued to love away the hurt turned hate that was mounting in the heart of this preacher's daughter.

I ran from His presence into the arms of the world, and spent the next two years bleeding and broken. Finally, I could take no more pain. I called to Him and said, "God, if you're real, show me your power." He had been waiting at my door all the time, longing to hear those words. Rapha walked in gently, but with great might, and commanded grief to loose its grip on my mind. Then He began to bind up my wounds. Over the next 72 hours, the Great Physician performed supernatural surgery, completely healing me with His presence, His word, and His blood.

I was still marveling at the healing when my father was diagnosed with prostate cancer. He exhaled for the last time less than a month later, sending air into the fresh wound in my side. Rapha watched me scramble for the love that my parents had provided, and He listened intently for another invitation to heal. But I kept silent. I wanted comfort more than wholeness so I ran into the arms of marriage. I married out of hurt and a desire to be loved, because I didn't know that only God could fill the void in me. The fourteen-year union ended in divorce, but yielded two of my life's greatest blessings, my children. They helped balm the heart of this single mother in ministry, but it would still take Rapha to heal such a debilitating wound.

I knew He could heal me, but I had become so familiar with wounds that I hardly knew how to function without them. They pampered my spiritual adolescence, justified my reasons for injuring others, and convinced me that realized purpose was only for the flawless.

I had learned to co-exist with wounds until Rapha interrupted that sham of a life with a question. "Sharon, do you want to be made whole?" He inquired. "Yes, Lord!" I responded. I started to prepare for another surgery, but this time He handed the scapula to me and told me to cut away the things that kept me wounded. If I was going to be healed this time, I would have to circumcise my own heart. And I would have to do so without the anesthesia of excuses.

I stared at Rapha for a long time and eventually took the scapula. I didn't yet know how to lay hands on myself, so He had to steady my palms. Then, one by one, I began to sever the attachments that kept me broken, and started to seal off those places with the blood of Jesus. The surgery was finally complete, but the assignment was just beginning. I didn't realize it at the time, but now I understand what Rapha was doing. He was making me a physician. He didn't just want to heal me; He wanted me to heal others. And if you're reading this, He wants the same for you.

Rapha has a message for you. He wants you to know that He is with you and that it is His will to heal you. He has a special word for those of you who have been wounded in ministry, but before you hear it, allow Him to hear you. Ask in faith for Him to heal you, and He will begin to bind up your wounds. He is troubling the waters of your heart with His word, but it's still up to you to jump in.

You're not the first one to wade in the waters of ministry or to feel overcome by the waves. Jesus already conquered those waters, and He teaches us how to rise above the seven wounds that many people in ministry experience: rejection, abandonment, loneliness, betrayal, dishonor, character assassination, and the effects of completion. By studying these wounds and the ways in which Jesus responded to them, we can better understand how to apply the blood that allows us to walk in supernatural healing in every area.

Rejection

He was despised and rejected of men. – Isa. 53:3

Jesus experienced rejection throughout His ministry, not only from religious leaders and unbelieving masses, but also from family members and followers (Jn. 7:5). Rejection is a spirit that inflicts damaging wounds in attempts to shift a person's life trajectory, and it tends to assault those in ministry before birth. That was certainly the case for Jesus. When Joseph learns that Mary is pregnant, he plans to have nothing to do with her or the child. He eventually accepts them in obedience to God's instruction, but his initial response is one of rejection. Rejection continues to accompany many unplanned pregnancies today. When thoughts about or attempts to abort a child occur, the spirit of rejection can access doors and use them for psychological torment for both the child and the parent. These doors can also open in the lives of some adopted children, and in children who feel deprived of close parental relationships (e.g. preachers' children).

Rejection can manifest in a number of ways. A few of them are: word curses, constant criticism, excessive physical punishment, child misuse (e.g. using children as pawns), child abuse or the tolerance thereof, the absence of affirmation, and demonstrating preference of one child over another. Those who struggle with rejection often feel unworthy, and have difficulty accepting love. Some are withdrawn and suspicious, choosing isolation over healthy relationships, while others use control and manipulation to maintain power without accountability. Almost all are driven by fear instead of love, and ironically, that fear perpetuates rejection.

Jesus overcame rejection by communing with the Father and remembering His identity. His closeness to the Father surpassed the pain of rejection, and kept Him from contaminating the relationships that were ordained for His life. Jesus used rejection to press into a deeper place of communion, and fellowship with the Father released a supernatural love that men had not seen. This means that, because Jesus was the essence of love, a new expression of His identity was revealed in the earth. When men rejected, He manifested. We must mirror His pattern. If we face rejection, we embrace the love and security of God. The love of God casts out fear, which is the base of all rejection, and it keeps us from being held captive by hurt. In turn, we align ourselves with the blood of Jesus by applying it to every place of rejection, and the blood will give us power to manifest the supernatural at a greater dimension.

Abandonment
My God, my God, why have you forsaken me? – Matthew 27:46

The Lion of Judah roars from Calvary's hill in the form of a question, and articulates the heartbreak of every minister who feels abandoned in the peak of ministry. Already dealing with the pain of disciples who fell asleep in Gethsemane and others who fell away during the arrest, Jesus chooses to complete the mission, even if He must do it alone.

Interestingly enough, the spirit of abandonment is never alone. It manifests after the operation of other spirits. For example, the spirit of addiction might be active in parents, but their addiction can lead to the physical and/or emotional abandonment of a child. Whether it comes from the absence of a person or of protection, abandonment assaults the sense of safety and makes the abandoned person feel unworthy of attention and care. This is why many people who have experienced physical abandonment find it easier to engage unhealthy or abusive relationships than those who have not. Although they may be independent in concrete areas (vocation, education, finance), those who have been abandoned are often very relationally dependent, and that dependency can cause clingy and even possessive behaviors.

People who have been emotionally abandoned tend to hide their feelings and discourage appropriate emotional responses (e.g.. "you don't have anything to cry about"). For them, making mistakes is unacceptable, having needs is a sign of weakness, being successful is necessary for worth, and exceeding expectations (no matter how inappropriate or unrealistic) is the best defense against abandonment. This perception allows abandonment to linger beneath the appearance of selflessness and relentless devotion, two qualities heavily celebrated in ministry. Many ministers who have experienced abandonment find value in rescuing others, so they flock to unhealthy situations to play the Messiah, saving the day but losing themselves while seeking to feel needed, appreciated, and secure.

Along with value, the spirit of abandonment attacks the believer's trust and willingness to commune. Communion is intimate presence, and it is especially needed during the absence of those whom we never anticipated would leave. As we continue to commune with God, His presence will heal the effects of abandonment and free us from its shadow. We also plead the blood of Jesus over the wound and flood it with the confessed word of God. By leaning into the One who will never leave or forsake us, we take part in our healing and shift from simply desiring wholeness to demonstrating it.

Loneliness

The Son of man has no place to lay his head. – Luke 9:58

Quick! Swallow that lump in your throat before someone sees it. It started rising after you left the pulpit and is steadily growing as you approach the car. Before you can buckle the seatbelt, it urges you to find someone, *anyone*, with whom you can share your heart. You scroll through your phone's contacts to no avail before finally admitting that you, like Jesus, have no place to lay your head.

We cannot study Jesus' life and ministry without observing the loneliness of leadership. He, more than anyone else, knew what it meant to be alone. He was alone in temptation in the wilderness; alone in faith on a boat; alone in prayer in a garden; alone in ministry on a cross. He faced loneliness long before it climbed into your passenger seat, so He can help you overcome it.

Loneliness begins by highlighting the lack of close relationships. This prompts sadness, emptiness, and a longing for contact in most people. Feeling isolated and deprived, they grow increasingly dependent on external relationships for a sense of wholeness and well-being. As this continues, loneliness begins to affect the body by raising blood pressure, inhibiting sleep quality, and causing over-exertion of heart muscles. The body literally struggles to rest when the heart is wounded by loneliness. The absence of close relationships affects every part of our being (spirit, soul, and body) because God fashioned us for fellowship.

Balancing the human need for relationships with a calling that does not always afford them can be painfully difficult. Sometimes, God uses loneliness to bring attention to areas in us that He has not fully saturated so He can fill us with more of His Spirit and power. Said another way, sometimes loneliness is a call to communion that allows fellowship with God to become the foundation of fellowship with people. Ministers who fail to heed this call can fall into depression, self-centeredness, idolatry, self-pity, and lethargy, all of which inhibit ministry and deepen the emotional wound.

When we study how Jesus dealt with loneliness, we are reminded of communion, or innermost fellowship, which can only occur when we know people by the spirit and not the flesh. To understand how Jesus overcame this, we must comprehend that loneliness doesn't necessarily denote a lack of people, or even a lack of those who genuinely love and honor a person. Rather, it is the result of experiences and interactions that are void of intimate knowing. We see this kind of experience when Philip asks Jesus to show the Father to the disciples. Jesus responds by saying, "Have I been so long time with you, and yet hast thou not known me, Philip? He that hath seen me hath seen the Father (Jn. 14:9)." Philip knew and loved Jesus from experience, but did not yet know Him by the spirit. Hence, his question was barren of understanding, and could have easily triggered loneliness. However, Jesus used it to teach the disciple how to access another level of fellowship with the Father. He knew that if Philip did not know how to commune with the Father, he would never be able to fully fellowship with the Son, and that is why Jesus couldn't take the absence of intimacy personally, although He knew that Philip was ordained to walk with Him. This attitude and insight made it impossible for Jesus to perpetuate loneliness.

To break the cycle of loneliness, there must be a renewed commitment to commune with God, because intimacy with Him is the only act that can relieve the heart of such a grave absence. When the pain of loneliness accosts us, we deal with it by taking those feelings to the Father. By refusing to carry or ignore that hurt, we unite faith with fellowship and trust God with what we cannot handle alone. As the Spirit of God begins to fill the voids exposed by loneliness, He resets our focus from scarcity to communion. This allows us to approach relationships in the right spirit, teaches us how to address loneliness without being subject to it, and sensitizes us to areas that we have not communed with God. As God changes our focus, He eases the pain and gives us a place to lay our head. Every time we commune with Him, we give the Lord a place to lay His head as well.

Betrayal

But Jesus said to him, Judas, betray you the Son of man with a kiss?
– Luke 22:48

Judas teaches us that betrayal typically comes with a kiss. Treachery cloaked in twisted affection, this spirit operates through the position of a trusted companion to inflict severe wounds to the side. It violates trust and intentionally causes harm, manifesting in unfaithful behaviors and approaches like infidelity, disclosure of private information, theft, participation in a person's demise, and dishonesty. Betrayal can leave behind damaged self-esteem, shock, self-doubting, anger, loss, grief, depression, and mental contamination. It can even trigger responses commensurate with Post Traumatic Stress Disorder (PTSD), a diagnosis given to many whose reaction to life-threatening events is a sense of intense helplessness, fear, or horror. This happens because betrayal threatens, at least to some degree, the very life of a person by placing his or her physical, social, political, financial, vocational, or ministerial existence in jeopardy.

Betrayal seems to come out of nowhere, but it actually arrives at key intersections of life. It arrives at junctures that force us to decide whether or not we will walk in destiny. Joseph's betrayal pushed him into rulership in Egypt; David's betrayal propelled him into kingship in Israel; and, Jesus' betrayal ushered Him into Lordship over heaven, earth, and even hell. Since betrayal threatens the life we know, it demands that we consider the life that God intended us to live.

Before Jesus was betrayed, He was already considering the life (and death) that God had intended for Him, and He had already chosen to accept it. For this reason, betrayal had no power to kill Him or wound Him so deeply that pain governed His decisions. So we learn from Him that the best response to betrayal is not reactive, but proactive, and that it always begins with a *"Yes, Lord."* Submission to God's will is not anticipation of betrayal, for we cannot operate out of fear, but rather, it is a willingness to walk in purpose – even if that road forks at a point of devastation. Those working through the pain of betrayal, especially in ministry, must begin with the blood of Jesus. His blood is applied to the heart and mind to prohibit hatred, bitterness, and vengeance from overtaking the person betrayed. It should also be applied to the memory to overcome revictimization, anxiety, and fear. The blood announces the fidelity of God to us, a devotion made visible precisely through His own wounds.

Dishonor

But Jesus said to them, a prophet is not without honor, but in his own country, and among his own kin, and in his own house.
– Mark 6:4

You're yesterday's news. People are used to seeing you flow in the spirit and they just expect you to preach them under the pew. You can get your own water and carry your own Bible; after all, you're just the son a carpenter. A lack of honor in the home, be it related to church or family, is the source of penetrating emotional wounds for many leaders in the ministry. The absence of honor is dishonor, and it first enters the mind and heart. If unaddressed, dishonor will bleed into words, actions, and ultimately, blatant displays of disrespect and degradation. Sometimes it joins complacency and familiarity, as we referenced above, and causes people to become so accustomed to their leader that they no longer revere the gift and anointing on his or her life. When this happens, God often uses a person outside of the ministry to bestow the appropriate level of honor on the leader so that honor can be restored to the House. For example, the anointing at Bethany displayed such a level of honor that it not only exposed the disciple's familiarity, but also continues to encourage believers to worship over 2,000 years later. Dishonor can also enter when people witness and respond inappropriately to the leader's humanity. To be sure, the leader is responsible for dealing with his or her humanity, but the disciple is responsible for responding to it out of divinity, *never* handling the leader out of the follower's flesh.

Most leaders who feel dishonored demonstrate one of two reactions: they accept and eventually perpetuate the dishonor of themselves, or they reject and dishonor others. Those who follow the first trend diminish their spiritual value to appease the carnal minds of those around them. They play small to avoid the appearance of pride and arrogance, but actually accommodate the spirit of dishonor and train their followers to do the same. Those who follow the second trend pour efforts into demonstrating their worth by constantly seeking glory. They tend to speak only of successes and achievements in hopes that the people who have not properly honored them will recognize their value. When the leader realizes that such boasting is futile, he often diminishes the value of others and attempts to pressure people into honor. When this happens, the people's actions may change, but their hearts will not. Forced honor is false honor.

Where there is no honor, there can be no promotion. The agenda of dishonor is to block physical and spiritual elevation, so unless we address it as Jesus did we cannot reach or operate at the level God ordained. Jesus always honored the Father and depended only on God to honor Him. Jesus did not belittle His identity, but He also never shamed those who could not see it. As we make honoring God our focus, He will not only confer honor upon us and cause others to do the same, but will also begin to heal the wound of dishonor. When we apply the blood of Jesus to the injury that came to hinder our advancement, God heals us, seals us, and promotes us to a greater level. Once we can fully occupy a new altitude, we know that we have been healed.

Character Assassination

Now the chief priests, and elders, and all the council, sought false witness against Jesus, to put him to death. – Matthew 26:59

Character assassinations are the emotional equivalent to physical crucifixions, and the most dangerous assassination attempts are led by religious leaders. Jealous or intimidated leaders may try to discredit the character, and therefore, the influence, of men and women of God who have been chosen for a specific assignment. Worst of all, they try to do so in the name of God. The best defense against character assassination is intimacy with the Lord. When the leader is on trial for his or her own assassination attempt, self-defense and explanation are of no value. This is why Jesus remained silent when accusations mounted against Him. Instead of talking to men, He spoke to the Father, and found a hiding place while on public display. To emulate His disposition is one of the greatest acts of faith, because it shows that we trust God with everything. Our lives are in His hands and we can't be plucked out. If we try to save ourselves, we will launch an internal struggle that draws strength from emotional wounds. That struggle has the capacity to shift us in profoundly harmful ways, which is why God often sends an attendant to help us in the fight.

If you are called to assist a spiritual leader, your assignment is to protect the leader's side. It is not your place to rectify their humanity. God does that. When you witness the leader's humanity, God is doing two things: He is trusting you to cover areas that could expose the leader to more wounds, and He is preparing you for promotion. Your promotion is contingent on your ability to protect God's anointed, even if the anointed person is the one attacking you. So, if you are right and the leader is wrong, it is not your place to justify your claim.

As long as you are righteous, the blood will speak for you. However, if you respond in offense or rebellion, and prompt a counter-attack on your leader, blood will be on your hands, and you will not be promoted.

You must remember that no attack is ever personal, no matter how intimate it seems. The attack is on what you represent and bring, which is liberty for your leader, and it is partly your responsibility to help the leader get free. Let me be clear. I am in no way saying that anyone should stay under leadership that is abusive, dangerous, or that puts others at risk. I am saying that when you know God has called you to a leader, encounters with his or her humanity are not justifications for your dismissal. If you can't handle their humanity, you can't handle God's divinity. And if you can't handle a character assassination, you're not ready for resurrection.

The Effects Of Completion
It is finished. – John 19:30

At some point, every leader must acknowledge when the assignment is complete. People who have gone through this know that fulfillment can mingle joy and agony. That is why so many leaders are unwilling to say it is finished. By lingering in places after the assignment is up, the leaders make themselves susceptible to debilitating wounds, and often injure others as a result. Some grow possessive out of insecurity, while others use micro-management to display power. For some, the pain triggered by a blank engagement calendar is unbearable, but for most, the hurt of blank stares from disciples who cannot carry the mantle proves even more excruciating. Still others wrestle when God transitions them from one assignment to another, from one people to another, because they will have to meet God and themselves all over again.

Some of the most difficult transitions come after great success, not after failure. It is Leaders can only be healed of wounds inflicted by the effects of completion by applying Jesus' response to their lives and His blood to their injuries. Jesus dealt with completion much like He did with betrayal – by preparing for and accepting it. Jesus prepared Himself by directing His attention, affection, and purpose toward the Father. He never separated His life from God's will, but made that life a manifestation of it. Jesus also prepared the disciples for the finished work by giving them power and authority to minister in His name, by speaking candidly with them about the effects of His departure, and by preparing the way for the Holy Spirit. On the cusp of His crucifixion, Jesus covered the disciples by praying over them, served the disciples by washing their feet, and gave Himself to the disciples by communing with them. Jesus knew that the ministry would continue after His death because it was centered on the Father. When wounded by the effects of a completed work, leaders must recommit to communing with and focusing on God, realizing that the blood of Jesus made us whole before we ever knew that we were wounded. As we do so, He will show us the vein of ministry that He desires us to flow in after the assignment is complete, knowing that our work for Him is of eternal consequence.

The work of the cross proclaims all that the blood has accomplished for us. It makes wombs of what used to be wounds to bring life from utter devastation, and manifests the original intent of Eden through a scarlet revelation.

Now there was about this time Jesus, a wise man, for he was a doer of wonderful works, a teacher. He drew over to him both many of the Jews and many of the Gentiles. And when Pilate, at the suggestion of the principal men amongst us, had condemned him to the cross, those that loved him at the first did not forsake him; And the tribe of Christians, so named from him, are not extinct at this day.

- Josephus, General in command of the Jewish forces of Galilee during the Great Revolt against Rome (66-73 C.E.)

CHAPTER 10

From Golgotha to Galilee

Forty days after the resurrection, we find ourselves on the shore of Galilee. He is here. We see His face, hear His voice, observe the mannerisms that we have come to know and love. He charges us to go before He begins to ascend, but we remain still, eyes fixed on the sky until an angel interrupts our gaze with a question, "Why are you standing here staring into heaven?"

The question continues to resound centuries later. Can you hear it? It reverberates in the hearts of those who want to shift from simply staring at the earth to having dominion over it. It dries the tears of disciples mourning the ascension and compels us to flow in the supernatural to advance God's kingdom. It pulsates in the minds of believers who refuse to wait until first Sunday to commune with God, who situate their lives in the scarlet stream of His blood. That same voice is calling to you, admonishing you to renounce the stale existence of mediocrity for a life of intimate fellowship.

If you're ready to respond, I'd like to offer some practical tools that will help you implement the principles and revelation covered in this book. We can begin by discussing ways to prepare for communion, since the body and blood of Jesus is the foundation of your new way of life. After this we'll examine sixty promises attached to the blood, as well as some decrees that target the specific areas that the blood restored. We will close with a final word from the Lord.

Preparing for Communion

Life begins at the Table. We, like believers in the early church, choose to partake of communion each day to remember the One who is life. Many churches only encourage communion when it is served in a religious setting and facilitated by an ordained person; and, while most of us observe these standards during communion for a corporate body, we also understand that the lack of a religious setting or ordination should not keep us from coming to the Table. Of course, we in no manner approach the Lord's Supper haphazardly. We always draw near with reverence for and assurance of Jesus' sacrifice, whether we are alone or with others.

We can prepare for personal communion by gathering unleavened bread (matza) and wine (or grape juice), each of which can be found at most grocery and health stores. If matza isn't available, plain crackers can be used as a substitute. After we prepare the items, we must prepare ourselves. We enter into communion with prayer and thanksgiving, as we remember the sacrifice that made fellowship with the Father possible. As we break the bread, we thank God that His broken body has strengthened our bodies to carry out His work without hindrance. When we prepare to drink the wine or juice, we acknowledge that the blood of Jesus avails everything we need, and we ask God to be for us what is most needed in that moment. For example, if pressures are great and stress is increasing, when we take communion we thank God for being our peace and our resting place. In so doing, we learn to fellowship with various parts of His person, and we invite Him to commune with us in every experience.

Along with taking communion on a daily basis, we should also do so during critical moments. If a major issue is at hand or we have to see immediate breakthrough, we need to commune with God all the more. Fellowshipping with Him in such crucial moments will cultivate intimacy and reduce alarm. In the case of a crisis or emergency, matza and juice may not be readily accessible. As we just mentioned, if we have to, we can use substitutes and still commune with God, because our faith is in His blood, not the physical elements themselves. This means that if we find ourselves in a hospital with saltine crackers and a carton of apple juice, we can still pray in faith, remember Jesus' sacrifice, and have intimate fellowship with God. This kind of intentional intimacy nurtures the lifestyle of communion that God originally envisioned for humanity, which is why we cannot unlock Eden without it. This revelation of communion is also our basis for understanding and applying the promises of God and the decrees that we make according to His word, for where His word is active, so is His blood.

A Promise is a Promise

The sixty promises that God made to Abraham apply to us today, for through the blood of Jesus and the faith of God, we who believe are the children of Abraham (Gal. 3:7). These promises accompany the blood covenant that expressed God's desire to commune with us.

As those who have been grafted into His lineage, we also confess these promises over ourselves and our descendants as we continue to walk in the spirit of communion and the essence of covenant.

1. I will make of thee a great nation. – Gen. 12:2
2. I will bless thee. – Gen. 12:2
3. I will make thy name great. – Gen. 12:2
4. Thou shall be a blessing. – Gen. 12:-2
5. I will bless them that bless thee. – Gen.12:3
6. I will curse him that curses thee. – Gen. 12:3
7. In thee shall all families of the earth be blessed. – Gen. 12:3
8. Unto thy seed will I give this land. –Gen. 12:7
9. For all the land which thou seest, to thee will I give it. – Gen. 13:15
10. (I will also give it) to thy seed for ever. – Gen. 13:15
11. And I will make thy seed as the dust of the earth. – Gen. 13:16
12. I will give it unto thee. – Gen. 13:17
13. He that shall come forth out of thine own bowels shall be thine heir. – Gen. 15:4
14. Look now toward heaven, and tell the stars, if thou be able to number them: and he said unto him, So shall thy seed be. – Gen. 15:5
15. And also that nation, whom they shall serve, will I judge. – Gen. 15:14
16. Afterward shall they come out with great substance. – Gen. 15:14

17. And thou shall go to thy fathers in peace. – Gen. 15:15
18. Thou shall be buried in a good old age. – Gen. 15:15
19. Unto thy seed have I given this land. – Gen. 15:18
20. And I will make my covenant between me and thee. – Gen. 17:2
21. I will multiply thee exceedingly. – Gen. 17:2
22. Thou shall be a father of many nations. – Gen. 17:4
23. I will make thee exceeding fruitful. – Gen. 17:6
24. I will make nations of thee. – Gen. 17:6
25. Kings shall come out of thee. – Gen. 17:6
26. I will establish my covenant between me and thee. – Gen. 17:7
27. (I will establish my covenant between me and) thy seed after thee in their generations for an everlasting covenant. – Gen. 17:7
28. (I will) be a God unto thee. – Gen. 17:7
29. (I will be a God) to thy seed after thee. – Gen. 17:7
30. I will give unto thee the land wherein thou art a stranger, all the land of Canaan, for an everlasting possession. – Gen. 17:8
31. (I will give) to thy seed after thee, the land wherein thou art a stranger, all the land of Canaan, for an everlasting possession. – Gen. 17:8
32. I will be their God. – Gen. 17:8
33. And I will bless her (Sarah). Gen. 17:16
34. I will give thee a son also of her. – Gen. 17:16

35. I will bless her (again). – Gen. 17:16

36. She shall be a mother of nations. – Gen. 17:16

37. Kings of people shall be of her. – Gen. 17:16

38. Sarah thy wife shall bear thee a son indeed. – Gen. 17:19

39. I will establish my covenant with him for an everlasting covenant. – Gen. 17:19

40. (I will establish my covenant) with his seed after him. – Gen. 17:19

41. I will make him (Ishmael) fruitful. – Gen. 17:20

42. I will multiply him exceedingly. – Gen. 17:20

43. Twelve princes shall he beget. – Gen. 17:20

44. I will make him a great nation. – Gen. 17:20

45. My covenant will I establish with Isaac. – Gen. 17:21

46. Sarah shall bear unto thee at this set time in the next year. – Gen. 17:21

47. I will certainly return unto thee according to the time of life. – Gen. 18:10

48. Sarah, thy wife, shall have a son. – Gen. 18:10

49. At the time appointed I will return unto thee. – Gen. 18:14

50. Sarah shall have a son. – Gen. 18:14

51. Abraham shall surely become a great and mighty nation. – Gen. 18:18

52. All the nations of the earth shall be blessed in him. – Gen. 18:18

53. Abraham will command his children and his household after him. – Gen. 18:19

54. (Abraham's children and household) shall keep the way of the LORD, to do justice and judgment. – Gen. 18:19

55. In Isaac shall thy seed be called. – Gen. 21:12

56. Also of the son of the bondwoman will I make a nation, because he is thy seed. – Gen. 21:13

57. In blessing I will bless thee. – Gen. 22:17

58. In multiplying I will multiply thy seed as the stars of the heaven, and as the sand which is upon the sea shore. – Gen. 22:17

59. Thy seed shall possess the gate of his enemies. – Gen. 22:17

60. And in thy seed shall all the nations of the earth be blessed. – Gen. 22:18

Speak Up: Decrees

Thou shall decree a thing and it shall be established unto thee: and the light shall shine upon thy ways. – Job 22:28

Now that we've reviewed what God has said, it's time to declare His word over our own lives. This happens through a decree. A decree is an authoritative order or decision to which individuals must comply. It is a proclamation or official statement made by a governing authority that has the force of law behind it. Spiritually speaking, a decree sets up boundaries and borders that safeguard against everything contrary to the promises of God.

According to Job 22:28, light shines when a decree is established. This truth infers that darkness can enter when no decree is issued. Just as the entire world was in darkness until the Lord issued a decree (Gen. 1), so are situations and circumstances until we speak up. Wherever there is darkness, we must release a decree to see what God has already promised. This principle also holds true for the seven areas that Jesus restored with His blood. In a moment we will examine decrees specifically related to these areas, but first, I'd like to decree some things over you and your generation. Through the power of Jesus' blood and the authority of His name, I decree and declare that:

- You will commune with God in every area that His blood has restored to you.
- The apostles and prophets, pastors and evangelists, teachers and saints in your generation will forsake mere religion and manifest the kingdom of God.
- Your churches and ministries will lead people to the Table, and not just the altar.
- Your disciples will rule faithfully, and utilize word and deed to shape the earth until it mirrors heaven.
- Your mothers and fathers will place the blood of Jesus on the doorposts of your era.
- Your sons and daughters will prophesy until the Spirit of God saturates all flesh.
- Your generation will seek God's face, demonstrate His power, and express His person to a world starving for a revelation of Him. And it will begin with you.

ARMED WITH THE TRUTH OF GOD, DECLARE THE FOLLOWING DECREES:

The Will

Zokef kefufim (God who straightens the Bent), Thank You that the blood of Jesus aligns my will with Your plans and desires for me. In the name of Jesus I decree that:

1. I am an expression of the life of Christ.

2. I am one with the Spirit of the Lord.

3. I have the mind of Christ.

4. I continuously renew my mind.

5. I have a heart for the things and people of God.

6. I want to do God's will.

7. I am willing and obedient.

8. I operate in the Spirit of wisdom, knowledge, and understanding.

9. I walk in Spirit of counsel and might.

10. I fear the Lord.

Health

Jehovah Rapha (God our Healer), Thank You that the blood of Jesus secures my healing and that of all my descendants. In the name of Jesus I decree that:

1. Every cell, muscle, organ, tissue and system in my body functions as God created it.

2. There are no malfunctions in my body.

3. The Spirit of Faith, who is my servant, comes with the manifestation of my healing.

4. I am healed by the stripes of Jesus.

5. The Word of God transforms my body and restores my health.

6. The Holy Spirit dwells in me and is sending life and healing throughout my body.

7. Every part of my body supports life and health.
8. I am anointed to lay hands on the sick and they will recover.
9. Along with salvation, God has already healed me and made me whole.
10. Supernatural life permeates my entire bodily system.

Wealth

Jehovah Chayil (Lord of Wealth), Thank you that you desire to prosper me and that it is your will and good pleasure to bless me. In the name of Jesus I decree that:

1. I possess everything God has already provided for me.
2. The blessing is upon me.
3. God has sent me to be a financial blessing to all the families in the earth.
4. Wealth and riches are in my house.
5. Every word spoken about my finances aligns with God's word so it cannot return to me void, but will accomplish the Lord's purposes and plans for my life and my generation.
6. My financial prosperity is independent of the world's system.
7. Every hindrance to my total prosperity is destroyed and dethroned.
8. The four winds of financial release have changed in my favor now.
9. I honor the Lord with my tithes, and every seed that I plant produces an exponential harvest.
10. The portals of heaven are open over me and they pour out vast blessings of abundance.

Authority

Adon Olam (Master of the World), Thank you that your blood gives me authority to facilitate the works of your hands, and makes my hands fit for the Master's use. In the name of Jesus I decree that:

1. All of the works of my hands are established and blessed.
2. I operate in purpose, power, and submission to the Lord.
3. I minister with demonstrations of power and of the Holy Spirit.
4. Fresh rain, anointing, and inspiration help me fulfill my purpose.
5. I fulfill the great commission.
6. I am strong in the Lord and in the power of His might to do His great work.
7. I use my God-given gifts and talents to help others and to honor God.
8. A legion of angels battles on my behalf to bring God's word to pass.
9. Miracles, signs, and wonders follow me.
10. Every prison of limitation in my life, generation, and ministry is totally eradicated.

Dominion

El-Elyon (The Most High God), I praise you as the sovereign ruler of all things, and thank you that you have given me dominion over the earth and power in the heavens. In the name of Jesus I decree that:

1. I am a partaker of God's divine nature.
2. I am a possessor of heaven and earth.
3. I am a part of the royal priesthood.
4. I am a co-creator.
5. I am above only and never beneath.
6. I am always first and never last.
7. I am victorious through Christ.
8. I am a visionary and a master-strategist.
9. I am a history-maker.
10. I am supernatural, and I operate in the miraculous for the glory of God.

Heart

El-Roi (The God Who Sees), Thank you that nothing in my heart escapes your sight, and that nothing in my life escapes your care. Just as you have healed my body, you have also healed my heart. In the name of Jesus I decree that:

1. I am not forgotten or forsaken. God remembers me.
2. I am the apple of my Father's eye.
3. I am the beloved, and I am worthy of love.

4. I am not alone.
5. I believe in God, so my heart is not troubled.
6. I am not abandoned or rejected.
7. I guard my heart with all diligence.
8. I am free of bitterness and unforgiveness.
9. I receive beauty for ashes.
10. I am safe and secure in the Lord.

Iniquity

Jehovah Tsidkenu (God Our Righteousness), Thank you that the blood of Jesus makes me the righteousness of God, and that it cleanses me of sin and allows me to receive every promise in your Word. In the name of Jesus I decree that:

1. I am saved by grace through faith.
2. I am a new creation in Christ Jesus.
3. I am redeemed from the curse of the law.
4. I am reconciled to God.
5. I am a son of God.
6. I am the righteousness of God in Christ Jesus.
7. I am forgiven of all sins because of the blood.
8. I am a saint.
9. I am a beneficiary of God's blood-covenant with Abraham.
10. I am free from condemnation.

Conclusion

Now you are ready and well able, because you have spent time at the Lord's Table. Go forth in the power of the blood and the purity of communion, never again listening to the lies that mediocrity tries to whisper in your ear. Bulldoze the high places that your old will constructed. Walk over the ruins of sickness and disease. Hoist a blood-stained banner over the demolition zone, and mark the place that abundance is transferred to you. Use your authority to advance the kingdom and shake the nations. Go! And this time, don't shake the dust off your feet. Make footprints of dominion to remind Satan that God has a ruler in the earth. While you walk, keep your precious heart in the hands of God. Love Him like it has never been broken. March boldly into your destiny without the weight of sin, carrying only the spirit of communion. Follow the scarlet stream that will always lead you back to the Table, to the place that God anoints you afresh with the oil of fellowship before sending you out again. So, fear not if you seem to lack the directions, confidence, or resources needed for this journey. As long as you have the oil, you have what you need to flow in Him. And as long as you have the blood, you have all you need to overflow.

NOTES

Chapter 1

1. James Strong. T*he Strongest Strong's Exhaustive Concordance of the Bible* (Grand Rapids: Zondervan, 2001), 1356.

2. Andrew Murray. "The Power of the Blood of Jesus." Accessed January 29, 2013. http://www.worldinvisible.com/library/murray/5f00.0572/5f00.0572.01.htm.

3. Walter Brueggemann. *The Prophetic Imagination* (Minneapolis: Fortress Press, 1989), 22.

4. Donald Lawrence. "Back II Eden," from The *Law of Confession, Part I.* Verity; 2009, compact disk.

Chapter 2

5. James Strong. *The Strongest Strong's Exhaustive Concordance of the Bible* (Grand Rapids: Zondervan, 2001), 1395.

6. In speaking about partaking of the body and blood of Jesus, we do not suggest transubstantiation, the theological belief that the elements of bread and wine are literally transformed into the body and blood of Jesus upon partaking of communion. Rather, we speak representatively, asserting that the power of these elements lies in their representation of the body and blood of Jesus.

7. Kevin J. Conner. *The Church in the New Testament* (Portland: BT Publishing, 1982), 293.

8. Edwin Friedman. *Generation to Generation: Family Process in Church and Synagogue* (The Guilford Press: New York, 2011), 124, 130.

NOTES

Chapter 3

9. L. Cilliers, L., "The History and Pathology of Crucifixion," *South African Medical Journal.* 93-12 (2003):938-41. http://www.ncbi.nlm.nih.gov/pubmed/14750495.

10. James Strong. *The Strongest Strong's Exhaustive Concordance of the Bible* (Grand Rapids: Zondervan, 2001), 1407.

11. Mohamed Omar Salem. "The Heart, Mind, and Spirit," http://www.rcpsych.ac.uk/pdf/ Heart,%20Mind%20 and%20Spirit%20%20Mohamed%20Salem.pdf

12. James Strong. *The Strongest Strong's Exhaustive Concordance of the Bible*, 1434.

13. Nancy Missler. "Seven Fold Spirit of God." Accessed May 25, 2013. http://www.khouse.org/articles/1996/121/.

14. James Strong. *The Strongest Strong's Exhaustive Concordance of the Bible*, 1525. Discussion of the refilling of the Spirit is influenced by study of the Greek *pleroo*, meaning "to be made complete" or "to fill up a hollow."

Chapter 4

15. Wounded healer phrase is inspired by Henry Nouwen's book, *The Wounded Healer*.

16. Robert M. Seltzer. *Judaism: A People and Its History* (New York: McMillan Publishing, 1987), 44.

17. Delbert R. Hillers. *Covenant: The History of a Biblical Idea* (Johns Hopkins Press: Baltimore, 1969), 101-105.

18. Claus Westermann. *Handbook to the New Testament* (Minneapolis: Augsburg Publishing, 1969), 4.

19. Jay Snell. "Why Physical Healing is in The Lord's Supper and How It Works To Heal You Now." Accessed January 29, 2013. http://jaysnell.org/Book9HTM/chapter_two.htm.

20. "Henrietta Lacks." Accessed February 17, 2013. http://en.wikipedia.org/wiki/Henrietta_Lacks

21. James Strong. *The Strongest Strong's Exhaustive Concordance of the Bible* (Grand Rapids: Zondervan, 2001), 1385, 1456.

22. "Jehovah Rapha." Accessed May 24, 2013. http://www.preceptaustin.org/jehovah_rophi__god_who_heals.htm.

23. James Strong. *The Strongest Strong's Exhaustive Concordance of the Bible* (Grand Rapids: Zondervan, 2001), *Ibid*, 1503.

24. John Sweet. "Healing." Accessed January 29, 2013. http://www.spiritualfoundations.com/Matthew/Chapter0 26Mat.htm.

Chapter 5

25. *Flowers and Plants*. "Plants with thorns, spines and prickles." Accessed March 12, 2013. http://www.flowers. org.uk/plants/whats-my-plant/plants-with-thorns-spines-and-prickles/.

26. *John 2*. "Matthew Henry's Commentary on the Whole Bible." Accessed March 2, 2013. http://mhcw.biblecommenter.com/john/2.htm.

27. Robert M. Seltzer. *Judaism: A People and Its History* (New York: McMillan Publishing, 1987), 60.

28. Word and Power Ministries. "Divine Substitution, Divine Exchange." Accessed January 29, 2013. http://www.wordandpower.us/Portals/3/pdf/Divine%20Exchange.pdf.

29. "The Hebrew meaning of Barak." Accessed March 17, 2015. http://biblehub.com/hebrew/1288.htm.

30. James Strong. *The Strongest Strong's Exhaustive Concordance of the Bible* (Grand Rapids: Zondervan, 2001), 1501.

31. *Ibid.*, 1498.

32. Bill Bailey. "Living in the blessing." Accessed May 25, 2013. http://www.wordoffaithworshipcenter.org/2009/03/.

Notes

Chapter 6

33. Varying accounts of nail placement stem from the ambiguity of the Greek word cheiras, which indicates anything below the forearm. Ancient accounts of nail placement in the palms do exist, but the weight of the condemned person's body could easily lead to the unfastening of nails from the hand. There are also reports of prisoners whose forearms or wrists were pierced, though no research can concretely assert the exact location of Jesus' nail prints. The aim of this depiction is not to argue one placement possibility over another, but to faithfully integrate available data, inasmuch is possible.

34. James Strong. *The Strongest Strong's Exhaustive Concordance of the Bible* (Grand Rapids: Zondervan, 2001), 1497.

35. *Ibid.*, 1541.

36. *Ibid.*, 1381.

37. *Ibid.*, 1498.

38. "God's Dunamis Power and Miracles." Accessed January 29, 2013. http://christianindiantv.homestead.com/ files/abq10.htm.

Chapter 7

39. James Strong. *The Strongest Strong's Exhaustive Concordance of the Bible* (Grand Rapids: Zondervan, 2001), 1453.

40. "Dominion Mandate." Accessed May 25, 2013. http://www.kingdomlife.org/blog/tag/ecclesiastes-3/.

41. James Strong. *The Strongest Strong's Exhaustive Concordance of the Bible*, 1511.

42. Material referenced here has been influenced by the teachings of Dr. Henry Malone, Doris Wagner, Chuck Pierce, Trever Dearing, David Wilkerson, et al.

43. "Introduction to Deliverance." Accessed May 25, 2013. http://www.vawtermark.com/introduction_to_ deliverance.htm.

Chapter 8

44. Servant of Messiah Ministries. "Sin, Transgression, and Iniquity." Accessed May 12, 2013. http://servantofmessiah.org/topical-studies/sin-transgression-iniquity/.

45. Rudi Swanepoel. "Transgressions and Iniquity." Accessed May 25, 2013. http://www.godsglory.org/devotional%20transgressions.htm.

46. Steve Bydeley. "Ancestral Iniquities." Accessed April 11, 2013. http://www.lapstoneministries.org/writings?iniquity.html.

47. Dale Sides. "Victory over Iniquity." Accessed May 24, 2013. http://www.lmci.org/articles.cfm? Article=14.

48. Steve Bydeley. Accessed April 11, 2013. http://www.lapstoneministries.org/writings/iniquity.html.

49. "Sin, Transgression, and Iniquity." Accessed March 23, 2013. http://servantofmessiah.org/topical-studies/sin-transgression-iniquity/.

Chapter 9

50. Dunkin Memorial Church. Inner Healing. "The Fruit of Rejection and Reasons for Rejection." Accessed April 20, 2013. http://isobbible.org/innerheal/InnerHealset/Session-Four.Html.

51. Claudia Black. "Understanding the Pain of Abandonment." Psychology Today, June 4, 2010. Accessed April 20, 2013. http://www.psychologytoday.com/blog/the-many-faces-addiction/201006/understanding-the-pain-abandonment.

52. Hara Estroff Marano. "The Dangers of Loneliness." *Psychology Today*, July 1, 2003. Accessed April 20, 2013. http://www.psychologytoday.com/articles/200308/the-dangers-loneliness.

Notes

53. Rachman, S. "Betrayal: A Psychological Analysis." *Behavior Research and Therapy* (2010): 304-11. Accessed April 20, 2013. doi: 10.1016/j.brat.2009.12.002.

54. Goldsmith, Rachel Evelyn. "Physical And Emotional Health Effects Of Betrayal Trauma: A Longitudinal Study of Young Adults." PhD diss, University of Oregon, 2004.

55. Lamia, Mary. "Shame: A Concealed, Contagious, and Dangerous Emotion." *Psychology Today*, April 4, 2011. Accessed April 20, 2013. http://www.psychologytoday.com/blog/intense-emotions-and-strong-feelings/201104/shame-concealed-contagious-and-dangerous-emotion.

Introductory Quote for Chapter 10

56. The Jewish Roman World of Jesus. "Josephus' References to Crucifixion." Accessed February 13, 2013. http://religiousstudies.uncc.edu/people/jtabor/cruc-josephus.html.

Chapter 10

57. Sharon Nesbitt. *Seeds: Decrees that Bring Dominion.* (2012), 8.

58. Cindy Trimm. *Commanding Your Morning: Unleash the Power of God in Your Life.* (Lake Mary: Charisma House, 2007), 129-132.

BIBLIOGRAPHY

Bailey, Bill. "Living in the Blessing." Accessed May 25, 2013. http://www.wordoffaithworship center.org/2009/03/.

Black, Claudia. "Understanding the Pain of Abandonment." *Psychology Today*, June 4, 2010. Accessed April 20, 2013. http://www.psychologytoday.com/blog/the-many-faces-addiction/201006/understanding-the-pain-abandonment.

Brueggemann, Walter. *The Prophetic Imagination*. Minneapolis: Fortress Press, 1989.

Burden, Larry. "Dominion Mandate." Accessed May 25, 2013. http://www.kingdomlife.org/blog/tag/ecclesiastes-3/.

Bydeley, Steve. "Ancestral Iniquities." Accessed April 11, 2013. http://www.lapstoneministries.org/writings/iniquity.html.

Cilliers, L. "The History and Pathology of Crucifixion." *South African Medical Journal*. 93-12 (2003):938-41. Accessed February 13, 2013. http://www.ncbi.nlm.nih.gov/pubmed/14750495.

Conner, Kevin J. *The Church in the New Testament*. Portland: BT Publishing, 1982.

Dunkin Memorial Church. *Inner Healing*. "The Fruit of Rejection and Reasons for Rejection." Accessed April 20, 2013. http://isob bible.org/innerheal/InnerHealset/Session-Four.Html.

Friedman, Edwin H. *Generation to Generation: Family Process in Church and Synagogue*. New York: The Guilford Press, 1985.

"God's Dunamis Power and Miracles." Accessed January 29, 2013. http://christianindiantv.homestead.com/files/abq10.htm.

Goldsmith, Rachel Evelyn. "Physical And Emotional Health Effects Of Betrayal Trauma: A Longitudinal Study of Young Adults." PhD diss, University of Oregon, 2004.

Hillers, Delbert R. *Covenant: The History of a Biblical Idea*. Baltimore: The Johns Hopkins Press, 1969.

BIBLIOGRAPHY

Lamia, Mary. "Shame: A Concealed, Contagious, and Dangerous Emotion." *Psychology Today*, April 4, 2011. Accessed April 20, 2013. http://www.psychologytoday.com/blog/intense-emotions-and-strongfeelings/201104/shame-concealed-contagious-and-dangerous-emotion.

Marano, Hara Estroff. "The Dangers of Loneliness." *Psychology Today*, July 1, 2003. Accessed April 20, 2013. http://www.psychologytoday.com/articles/200308/the-dangers-loneliness.

Missler, Nancy. "Seven Fold Spirit of God." Accessed May 25, 2013. http://www.khouse.org/articles/1996/121/.

Murray, Andrew. "The Power of the Blood of Jesus." Accessed January 29, 2013. http://www.worldinvisible.com/library/murray/5f00.0572/5f00.0572.01.htm.

Nesbitt, Sharon. *Seeds: Decrees that Bring Dominion*. 2012.

Nouwen, Henri J.M. *The Wounded Healer: Ministry in Contemporary Society*. New York: Doubleday, 2010.

Oxford Bible Church. "Healing Promises." Accessed January 29, 2013. http://www.oxfordbiblechurch.co.uk/pages/teachings/healing/101.php.

Precept Ministries International. "Jehovah Rapha." Accessed May 24, 2013. http://www.precept austin.org/jehovah_rophi_ _god_who_heals.htm.

Rachman, S. "Betrayal: A Psychological Analysis." *Behavior Research and Therapy* (2010): 304-11. Accessed April 20, 2013. doi: 10.1016/j.brat.2009.12.002.

Roman Crucifixion. "The Horror of Roman Crucifixion." Accessed February 13, 2013. http://www.lillenas.com/vcmedia/2401/2401385.pdf.

Seltzer, Robert M. *Judaism: A People and its History*. New York: McMillan Publishing, 1987.

Seltzer, Robert M. *Jewish People, Jewish Thought: The Jewish Experience in History.* New York: McMillan Publishing, 1980.

Servant of Messiah Ministries. "Sin, Transgression, and Iniquity." Accessed May 12, 2013. http://servantofmessiah.org/topical-studies/sin-transgression-iniquity/.

Sides, Dale. "Victory over Iniquity." Accessed May 24, 2013. http://www.lmci.org/articles.cfm? Article=14.

Snell, Jay. *Healing, Prosperity, and Family Well Being.* "Why Physical Healing is in The Lord's Supper and How It Works To Heal You Now." Accessed January 29, 2013. http://jaysnell.org/Book9HTM/chapter_two.htm.

Strong, James. *The Strongest Strong's Exhaustive Concordance of the Bible.* Grand Rapids: Zondervan, 2001.

Swanepoel, Rudi. "Transgressions and Iniquity." Accessed May 25, 2013. http://www.godsglory.org/devotional%20transgressions.htm.

Sweet, John. "Healing." Accessed January 29, 2013. http://www.spiritualfoundations.com/Matthew/Chapter026Mat.htm.

"The Hebrew Meaning of Barak." Accessed March 17, 2015. http://biblehub.com/hebrew/1288.htm.

Trimm, Cindy. *Commanding Your Morning: Unleash the Power of God in Your Life.* Lake Mary: Charisma House, 2007.

The Analytical Greek Lexicon. Grand Rapids: Zondervan Publishing, 1967.

The Jewish Encyclopedia. "Crucifixion." Accessed February 12, 2013. http://www.jewishencyclopedia.com/articles/4782-crucifixion.

The Jewish Roman World of Jesus. "Josephus' References to Crucifixion." Accessed February 13, 2013. http://religiousstudies.uncc.edu/people/jtabor/cruc-josephus.html.

BIBLIOGRAPHY

The Layman's Parallel Bible. Grand Rapids: Zondervan Bible Publishers, 1973.

Vawtermark Ministries. "Introduction to Deliverance." Accessed May 25, 2013. http://www.vawtermark.com/introduction_to_deliverance.htm.

Westermann, Claus. *Handbook to the New Testament.* Minneapolis: Augsburg Publishing, 1969.

Word and Power Ministries. "Divine Substitution, Divine Exchange." Accessed January 29, 2013. http://www.wordandpower.us/Portals/3/pdf/Divine

About the Author

Dr. Sharon R. Nesbitt is the founding Pastor and Apostle of Dominion World Outreach Ministries, a multi-racial, non-denominational ministry located in Marion, Arkansas. By using her gifts to equip, train and release believers to fully operate in their God-given purpose, Dr. Nesbitt is quickly becoming a leading voice in the move to re-establish God's kingdom agenda and to manifest the supernatural ministry of Christ in the earth.

Dr. Nesbitt strives to positively influence the lives of God's people through the application of the Word. Her sensitivity to the needs of people and her God-given vision to reach the nations has prompted the establishment of several organizations, some of which are Dominion World Development Corporation, an outreach organization with a global focus, and Dominion Bible School, an educational center in Guatemala City, Guatemala, that trains disciples for ministry in rural regions of that country. While sustaining international exploits, Dr. Nesbitt also leads projects devoted to kingdom enterprise. She has directed the acquisition, purchase and development of land and facilities on behalf of the ministry without the aid of financial institutions; the most recent acquisition being the purchase of 52 acres that will house the new Dominion campus.

Dr. Nesbitt travels extensively for business and ministry to manifest the kingdom of God in strategic spheres. In teaching and preaching the word of God with miraculous demonstrations of power, the mother of two challenges believers to walk in dominion by accessing and operating in new levels of faith. As she ministers throughout the nation and the world, Dr. Sharon Nesbitt continues to plant supernatural seeds that will yield a harvest for generations to come.

Additional Information

Requests for additional product information can be relayed through the following mediums:

Dominion World Outreach Ministries
3700 Interstate 55 North
Marion, AR 72364
www.dominionworld.org
info@dominionworld.org
Phone: (866) 579-5807
Fax: (870) 739-1332

Other Works By Dr. Sharon Nesbitt

Seeds: Daily Decrees That Bring Dominion

Chosen For Greatness: Discovering Your Dominion Mandate

Setting the Captives Free: Deliverance Training Manual